To: Meg

May Gods f JN

you now and forever, and may your
gifts continue to bless all
whom he allows you to serve.

Rev Dr. Ella McDonald

GREAT
DIVERSITIES

BLACK, FEMALE AND A PREACHER; SERMONIC STRATEGIES FOR OVERCOMING RESISTANCE TO GAINING A HEARING IN VARIOUS CULTURAL SETTINGS

REV. DR. ELLA M. MCDONALD

"GREAT DIVERSITIES"

Black, Female and a Preacher;
Sermonic Strategies for Overcoming Resistance to
Gaining a Hearing in Various Cultural Settings

Reverend Dr. Ella M. McDonald

Great Diversities: Black, Female and a Preacher; Sermonic Strategies for Overcoming Resistance to Gaining a Hearing in Various Cultural Settings.

Copyright © 2018 by Reverend Dr. Ella M. McDonald

ISBN-13:978-1718658592
ISBN-10:1718658591

Catalogued in the Library of Congress

This book was printed in the United States of America.

Published by:
True Faith Consulting & Publishing

All Rights Reserved. No part of this book may be reproduced or transmitted in any form or by any means, electronically or mechanically, including photocopying recording, or by any other information storage and retrieval system, without written permission in writing from the Author.

Unless otherwise noted, all Scripture quotations are taken from the King James Version Bible.

Dedication

In remembrance of my grandparents, Mr. E. J. Martin and Mrs. Ella Mae Martin, who adopted me, nurtured me, and loved me! As poor as they were, they made certain that I received an opportunity to pursue a higher education.

I also want to dedicate this book to my great nephew Jaellan Jeremiah Wheeler, who was always in my arms loving me like no one else could the whole time the vision of this book was developing.

Acknowledgement

As I was preparing to graduate from Perkins School of Theology, on the campus of Southern Methodist University, in Dallas. Texas, I had no idea what I would use as a Theme for my project. But, as He always does, God provided me with a "ram in the bush". My Supervisor, Dr. Alyce McKenzie presented me with the topic: *"Black, Female, and a Preacher."* I thought about her topic for a couple of days and decided, why not? I am black! No one can change that. I am a female! No one can change that. I am a preacher! God called me to that. And, I will fight for it all my life! As a black female preacher, I have faced resistance my entire career as a minister. So, I thought I would share my struggles and my accomplishments based on the experiences I have endured.

The purpose of this book is not intended to give you tools for higher academic debate or argue as to whether women have been called to preach. This book was written to share things that have been accomplished and or defeated in the journey of women toward ministry. I am certain you have read or heard similar ideas given in many ways. I have suffered in countless ways that should have sent me running, but the fact that you are reading this book is evidence that I am still here!

By the grace of God, I have been given so many friends that have shared their time, money, words of confidence, expressions of love and encouragement. I must acknowledge their support. To the Professors of Perkins School of Theology that displayed interest in me and provided me with aid and support: Dr. Alyce McKenzie, Dr. Jeanne Stevenson-Moessner, Dr. Thomas Span, Dr. Theo Walker, Dr. Gary MacDonald, Dr. Paula Dobbs - Wiggins, Dr. Elaine Heath and Dr. Michael Waters.

To my friends who spent many hours editing the written work of my D.Min. project: Mrs. Nancy Summers,

Mrs. Cynthia Wilson, Ms. Susan Chamberlain, and Ms. Dianna Thompson. With the help of these ladies, I only had to present the manuscript once.

I must also thank Ms. Beverly Gilmore for caring enough to share with Mrs. Elgie Loyd, my need for an editor and publisher. Because of her, this book gained hope again! Likewise, I owe much gratitude to Agape Temple AME Church, Rockwall FUMC, St. Luke AME Church, Gaines Chapel AME Church, Mabank First UMC, Mesquite First UMC, and The Iglesias de Independencia Church. These churches, not only open their doors and allowed me to preach, but also permitted their congregation to take the survey.

To my good friends who nursed and encouraged me to not give up during my period of sickness: Mrs. Susan Crowell, Mrs. Theresa Crewse, Mrs. Rosie Alexander, Mr. Kirk Ragsdale, Mrs. Susan Sharp and Mrs. Linda Whitaker. I express my most sincere love and dedication. Thank you so much for being there with me! Finally, I must thank Mr. Guy and Mrs. Brenda Hargrave, who gave me a place to escape when things got tough. There are countless other friends that have enhanced my growth throughout my ministry, but I would have to write another book to hold their names and to express my appreciation towards them!

Rev. Dr. Ella M. McDonald, M.Div., D. Min
St. Luke AME Church Waco, Texas

Table of Contents

APPENDICES

Introduction

In February 1993, I experienced my first encounter with race and ministry. I was asked to do a presentation on diversity at McKinney High School in McKinney Texas. At the time, I had been teaching math at this school for sixteen years. I had been very successful at taking mathematical facts and explaining them to a diverse classroom of students in such a way that they were able to understand mathematics. Because I love teaching, mathematics, and the students, I was able to take these mathematical facts and relate them to the students in such a way that it was relevant to them as human beings. This was a gift from God that brought me much success as a high school math teacher.

As a teacher, I was patient, kind and understanding. Students of all races and ethnicities loved being in my class, and I received great praise from them. Because they would talk positively about me to each other and to their parents; parents would write letters of appreciation to the principal of the school on my behalf. This made the principal take notice of my potential and increased her interest in me as a leading teacher. When the school decided to start a school-within-a-school for at-risk students, she asked me to become the head of that department. I accepted the challenge and was able to share my strategies and techniques with three other teachers--a science teacher, a history teacher and an English teacher--who were assigned to work with me in this Project. Our school-within-a-school became so successful that we were asked to travel to other cities to introduce to them our curriculum and teaching strategies. As a presenter, each time I gave the presentation, I received many compliments and words of encouragement.

After one of these tours, my principal told me that the observing principal at the other school had asked her if he could trade her one of his teachers in exchange for me. I thought that was funny at the time. However, I discovered later that it was not my knowledge that had attracted the principal. What these observers were attracted to was my experiential, emotional approach to speaking, teaching and leading. In other words, my self-awareness of what I was feeling, and thinking was being demonstrated through the way I expressed, guided, controlled and directed my emotional impulses. My understanding of the dynamics of the room enabled me to affect the emotions and behavior of this group of teachers in an optimistic and positive way. My emotional behavior generated emotions in these teachers that, in turn, dictated a motivational response that resulted in their eagerness to give this program a try.

Because of the responses and feedback from the tours, my principal began to take notice of my speaking ability. This led her to invite me to participate as facilitator on a panel of teachers who were speaking at our school's in-service training on the topic of diversity in the classroom. At first, I was very hesitant because, while I knew a lot about teaching mathematics, diversity was not a topic in which I had any formal training or education. However, after a lengthy conversation with the principal, she convinced me that this was exactly what I had already been talking about for four months.

On the day that I was to make this presentation, I had no idea what I was going to say. So, I made up my mind that I would just show up and talk about how I felt as a child when I experienced the integration of public schools in the early 1960's. When it was my time to speak, I followed a teacher who was both a coach and a history teacher. His presentation involved a demonstration of how he started each morning of class by greeting and shaking the hands of his students. When he got to me, he said, "Good morning, how are you?" while he was still holding the hand of the man next to me and congratulating him on a great football game Friday night. The teacher was a White man, I was a Black woman, and the man next to me was a White man. This teacher never once looked at me. He greeted me while still looking at, and holding the hand of, the White man who sat beside me. This action made me feel invisible and insignificant. Afterward, I did not want to hear anything else he had to say.

The teacher's intention was to demonstrate how he participated in the students' lives and how he congratulated them on their achievements; however, his action revealed a lack of sensitivity. As a Black female, his oversight of my race, gender and ethnicity in the room was offensive and unappreciated. When it was my time to speak and after I was introduced, another teacher made the following comment: "Ella, you going to tap dance or sing for us?" My response was, "Neither!" Knowing I was not very accepting of that comment, to bail the first teacher out of a difficult situation, another teacher tried to justify his statement with comments about how gifted Blacks are in dancing and singing and entertaining. I was still not amused. However, my ability to empathize with the emotions of the other members of that group and have insight on their thought processes afforded me the ability to see where I fit in that group. So, I began my presentation by talking about stereotypes and oversights. God used me so well that day that those teachers who were coming to the second session wanted to make sure they arrived in time to get a seat in my session. I left work that day feeling confident that God had used me to make a difference.

Because I am an experiential emotional person, I wanted to extend this grace into my preaching ministry. According to an essay written by Joel R. Beeke, in the book *Feed My Sheep: A Passionate Plea for Preaching*:

> The term experimental comes from the Latin experimentum, meaning "trial." It is derived from the verb experior, meaning "to try, proving, or putting to the test." That same verb can also mean "to find or know by experience," thus leading to the word experiential, meaning knowledge gained by experience[1]

My desire to experience this gift was granted in June 1995, when I was given an opportunity to attend a Walk to Emmaus, which is a spiritual retreat led by an ecumenical community of Christians. This was the first time that I had been in an ecumenical worship setting, and I noticed several things about this community. The first thing that I noticed was that even though the songs were unfamiliar to me, the song lyrics were very inspiring. The next thing that I noticed was the diversity of the speakers. There were both male and female clergy with representation of the White, Hispanic and Black cultures and communities. With the exception of the Black clergywoman, whom I was certain was doing everything she could to restrain her usually emotional preaching style, all the speakers spoke in their own traditional manner; and I received something from each of their messages.

---

[1]Eric Alexander, Joel Beeke, James M. Boice, Sinclair Ferguson, Don Kistler, John MacArthur, Albert Mohler, John Piper, R.C. Sproul, Jr., and Derek Thomas, *Feed My Sheep: A Passionate Plea for Preaching* (Soli Deo Gloria Publishers, Florida 2002) p. 95.

After I got over the anxiety of worrying about whether I would be called on to give one of these talks spontaneously, the desire to experience what I had just observed became overwhelming. My next inspiration came when I experienced the powerful and spiritual way in which communion was served. Never had I felt that way about receiving communion. As a result of this worship experience, my understanding of the giving and receiving of the elements of the table of the Lord was elevated to a new spiritual height. Dr. Alyce McKenzie gave an excellent description of this event in her sermon "Joy for the Journey:

Reflections on the Walk to Emmaus," Luke 24:13-35.

She writes:

> The plot of the walk to Emmaus scene epitomizes the plot of the whole Gospel of Luke (and, for that matter, of John). Jesus is our companion on the way, but we do not recognize him. The astounding tale of the women had not been enough to kindle these two men's faith. Their recognition of Jesus comes when "he took bread, blessed, and broke it" (24:30). In that moment, recognition dawned. In that moment they had a change of heart: from being "slow of heart to believe" (24:25) to having hearts that burned within them as he spoke to them on the road (24:32).[2]

I enjoyed this spiritual retreat and was motivated to want to minister outside of the walls of my local congregation.

---

[2]Dr. Alyce McKenzie, Joy for the Journey: Reflections on the Walk to Emmaus (Malankara World St. Basil's Syriac Orthodox Church, Ohio 2009-2014) http://www.malankaraworld.com//Library/Sermons/_3rd-sunday-after-new-sunday-AMMM.htm.

I inquired about how to become a part of this community. Within four months, I was invited to serve as clergy on my very first Walk to Emmaus team. As I look back on these events in my life, I see a pattern in which God was preparing me for a new level of ministry. He used my experiential and emotional approach to teaching as a tool which opened the doors of opportunity for me to present my teaching strategies to other educators in different communities. The success from this experience gave me an opportunity to present a message to a group of teachers on the topic of the difference between diversity and deficiency. The response from this presentation motivated and elevated my self-esteem to a new perspective on my purpose and direction for life and inspired me to publish this book.

The next step in my preparation was for me to experience leading an ecumenical spiritual retreat which revealed to me how this new gift of exhortation could be used to further my ministry in the Kingdom of God. Finally, I was ready to walk through those open doors of opportunity to facilitate and preach in conferences, retreats, and worship services in which I was often the only Black person present. I felt comfortable and accepted in this venue. Conversely, while preaching in other cultural contexts, because my approach to preaching is experiential and emotional, that approach would sometimes be seen as problematic. My style of preaching along with my gender and race were often the root of resistance that prevented me from being taken seriously as an agent of God from the pulpit. My messages were often denigrated as "little talks" or "great speeches" rather than taken seriously as sermons. Instead of being heard as life-changing messages, they were sometimes viewed as emotional, motivational and entertaining.

As a Black female whose approach to preaching is experiential and emotional, being called an entertainer is an insult that can cast shadows on my credibility as an agent of God's communication. These shadows include three things: fear, doubt and uncertainty. When one lives in these shadows, they can cause emotional low self-esteem to make one question her worth, values, and usefulness as anointed vessel to be used by God. This lack of confidence in credibility can show up as a resistance that hinders a Black female preacher from gaining a hearing from the pulpit. In Proverbs 9:10, the Bible says, "The fear of the LORD is the beginning of wisdom, and knowledge of the Holy One is understanding."

Fear in this sense does not mean fright. Here, the word fear means respect. In order to preach Christ-centered messages with a desire to lift the Sovereignty of God above humanity, one must give God the respect God deserves. Thus, while fear is normal, the problem with fear is that it can make one reluctant to continue ministry. In other words, the fear of disappointing or failing to please God sometimes causes an experiential preacher to defer his/her desire to walk in the authority that has been given to him/her by God as an agent of God's communication. This deferment often will last until she/he has heard from God through some type of personal experience. An example of this can be found in 1 Kings Chapter 19. In this passage we find Elijah, after doing what he thought was the will of God, discouraged and hiding in a cave. Jezebel had threatened his life, and he could not feel the presence of God.

Not being able to experience the presence of God causes him to fear that God is not with him, so he runs to a place where God had once appeared to Moses in hopes that God might appear there to him also. In the meantime, Elijah tells God "I have had enough." I contend that Elijah was not only afraid of Jezebel, he was also afraid that he had failed to do the will of God. Feeling alone, frightened and defeated, Elijah was ready to abandon his ministry. Living under the shadow of fear, doubt and uncertainty, his lack of confidence became a resistance that affected Elijah's desire to continue preaching and teaching. This cast a shadow over his ministry that caused him to believe that it would be better to run from the call of God on his life than to risk his life trying to convert people who did not want to be converted.

For an experiential preacher, one who gains knowledge of the scriptures by experience, how one experiences the truth of the Christian Doctrines of the church can be more meaningful than the theology of the doctrine. This contrasts with those who gain knowledge through a more conceptual, linear approach in which the appeal is directed more towards the intellect and reasoning of the hearer. So, while I gave those who viewed my sermons as "little talks" or "great speeches" a pass, I knew I had failed as an agent of God to fulfill my assignment. For you see, the assignment of an experiential, emotional preacher is not to entertain; it is to proclaim a Christ-center message that tells the Gospel truth of the offer of salvation extended to all by God through the grace of Jesus Christ. The only desired response the experiential preacher seeks is that those who hear their message will accept this offer of salvation. If a Black female preacher preaching a Christ-centered message and seeking to gain a hearing in and beyond her own cultural context is going to overcome these resistances, she must develop sermonic strategies that will encourage her to pursue her ministry no matter what she might face along the way. Which makes this book so important to me as I share the experience of my journey through this project.

The purpose of this project practicum is to identify, form and field-test sermonic strategies to equip Black female preachers to overcome resistance to their challenging message, both in and beyond their cultural setting. The project practicum was conducted over a six-month period in which I preached the same message in five diverse cultural settings: a multi-cultural setting that was seventy- five percent Black; a multi-cultural setting that was ninety percent White; a predominantly Black congregation; a predominantly White congregation; and a predominantly Hispanic congregation. As a final test, I created a Unity in Diversity worship service in which another Black female preacher preached the sermon.

My Book includes a written objective evaluation of each of the five sermons preached, interviews with three Black female preachers who pastor in a cultural context other than their own, evaluations from an advisory team of two female clergy and four laypersons who offered their opinions of what they experienced in observing my experiential emotional preaching strategies in various cultural contexts, a written evaluation of the opinions of volunteers from various cultural settings of the diversity unity service, and finally, based on the collected information from all evaluations, a conclusion about the preaching strategies' usefulness in helping other Black female preachers overcome resistance to gaining a hearing. Using these sources, it is my prayer that this Book will contribute valuable insight towards my desire and calling to become an effective preacher in and beyond cultural context. I also pray that my Book will provide valuable resources that will help other Black female preachers to preach messages centered on the life, death and resurrection of Christ that will be accepted in settings of diverse cultural contexts.

The following are clarifications and definitions of words that I feel need explaining, because they may mean different things to people of diverse cultures. These are important terms used in this Book:

1. Resistance is the opposition facing women who preach God's Word.

2. Preaching strategies are approaches to preaching that cross-cultural lines.

3. Logical is a component of preaching that is compelling and coherent.

4. Linear is a sequential and intellectual understanding of biblical material.

5. Agents of God's communication are preachers who seek to be faithful interpreters of God's Word.

6. Form and field-test preaching insights means to develop a practice and try it out.

7. Black Church tradition is worship that mainly emphasizes the assurance of individual liberation and transformation.

8. Black preaching style is a style of preaching that allows the preacher to have the freedom to be creative in every aspect of the delivery of the sermon.

9. Christ-centered preaching is preaching centered around the life, death and resurrection of Christ.

10. Whooping is a celebratory style of Black preaching that uses chanting, melody and call-and-response that pastors typically use to close a sermon

11. Experiential preaching is Christ-centered preaching that stresses the importance of a personal faith in the works of Christ learned through the spiritual knowledge of the truth presented in scripture.

12. The Walk to Emmaus is an ecumenical spiritual renewal program for both men and women intended to strengthen the local church through the development of Christian disciples and leaders.

13. Call and response is a Black cultural climactic style of dialogical preaching.

I see my calling as a Black female preacher as one of spreading the good news of Christ to all people. If I am to communicate the Word of God effectively, I must learn to preach effectively across cultures. Working in another culture with your own cultural values can be frustrating and counterproductive; so, the preacher needs to develop some sermonic strategies that might help him/her to overcome the resistance he/she might face. Thus, it is my hope that this Book combines my experiential emotional approach to preaching with a more conceptual liner approach to preaching that might be used to enhance my preaching skills when preaching in various cultural contexts. I further hope that what I have learned will be helpful to others.

Chapter 1

Biblical and Theological Approach

Introduction

When I was a child of eleven months, I was abandoned by both of my parents. Thus, for most of my life I have struggled with issues of identity, alienation, separation and reconciliation. I have often found myself searching beyond my home and cultural setting in a quest to find significance for my life and to fill the emptiness that I felt within my soul. I was lost and searching for identity. God was not talked about in the home in which I was brought up, so although I had heard that there was a God, I never knew what that meant. Further, while I realized something was missing in my life, I absolutely did not know what it was or where to find it. The one thing I did know for sure was that I longed for love and a sense of belonging.

Somehow, through watching the movie, "The Wizard of Oz," I seemed to find a connection and a temporary comfort. In this movie, the character Dorothy found herself lost and separated from what she called home. In her search to find her way back there, she was convinced by the people of Oz that if she went to see the Wizard, he could help her return to her loved ones. For 21 years of my life, I too was "off to see the Wizard, the wonderful Wizard of Oz, because of the wonderful things he does." I knew that the movie was fiction and that there was no Wizard who could give me that kind of fulfillment, but I sure hoped for it. Later in life, I realized it was Dorothy's successful journey from separation to reconciliation that gave me a sense of hope that one day I would be reconciled with people who loved and wanted me. To receive this reconciliation, Dorothy first had to believe that the Wizard existed. Dorothy believed and followed the yellow brick road to see him. But in the end the Wizard left without her. It wasn't until Dorothy put her faith in the unknown and believed that she had the power to get home on the inside of her, that she finally woke up and found herself at home.

Like Dorothy, my hope in the Wizard was eventually replaced, though for me it was by my faith in the existence of a loving God. As an abandoned child, the search for love was an ever-present activity in my life. My final attempt to search for this love was through marriage. When this experience failed, the circumstances of my life compelled me to go to church. I was in church, but I had no idea what was happening. At that time, I was completely ignorant of God's presence in Jesus Christ, and I surely did not know anything about God's offer of a life-giving relationship or how to experience this relationship through the Church. I went to church one Sunday because my husband was going, but on that Sunday, I had an unusual experience that moved me to join that church. After that experience, I went to church on a regular basis for about two months, and then I quit.

There was a lady in the congregation, named Willie Frances McAdams, who saw me and took interest in me. When I stopped attending, for some reason it appeared that everywhere I looked, there she was, talking about "you better come to church." I could be at a stop sign, and I would hear a car horn, and when I looked, there she was talking about "you better come to church." I would be in the grocery store buying groceries, and she would be there talking about "you better come to church." I would be out on the dance floor at the night club, and she would be there talking about, "you better come to church." So, finally, I got a chance to ask her why. And for the first time in my life, somebody told me the story of God and his Love for me.

She told me that Jesus died for me so that I might have a loving relationship with God. She explained to me how that relationship was a relationship of love and self-giving. I still did not fully understand, but I knew there was something inside of me that was longing for that kind of relationship. In fact, I could not get it off my mind. It weighed so heavily on my mind that I thought about it night and day. What I know now is that the reason that I was thinking about this so much was because God was pressing the issue. God wanted to have a personal encounter with me. I could not stop thinking about this love of God because my heart, mind and soul were being nudged and influenced by God's Holy Spirit to receive the gift of eternal life through the grace of Jesus Christ. Eventually, by faith, I accepted the love of God and put my trust in God to help me apply this faith to all my relationships with family, church and the world.

> **Thus, I begin this Book by declaring that I believe God exists.**

In his book *Delighting in the Trinity: An Introduction to the Christian Faith*, Michael Reeves states:

> I could believe in the death of a man called Jesus, I could believe in his bodily resurrection, I could even believe in a salvation by grace alone; but if I do not believe in this God, then, quite simply, I am not a Christian. And so, because the Christian God is triune, the Trinity is the governing center of all Christian belief, the truth that shapes and beautifies all others. The Trinity is the cockpit of all Christian thinking.[3]

If I agree with this argument of Michael Reeves, that to be a Christian I must believe in God, then I say that I am a Christian. Because I am a Christian, I also believe in the life, death and resurrection of Jesus Christ which grants me eternal life. The Bible says it this way, "And this is life eternal, that they might know thee the only true God, and Jesus Christ, whom thou hast sent" (John 17:3). Therefore, my theological position is that through the love of the triune God, people are restored and reconciled to a loving relationship with God and each other.

Theological Position

My theological position acknowledges a triune God. According to Webster's New World College Dictionary, the word *triune* means "three in one; constituting a trinity in unity, as the Godhead."[4] The Trinity is one of the distinctive doctrines of Christianity. It is a doctrine that refers to God as three distinctive persons, who is only one divine being, which is God. For the most part, the doctrine of the Trinity is very mysterious and difficult to comprehend.

Michael Reeves, Delighting in the Trinity: An Introduction to the Christian Faith, Downers Grove, IL, InterVarsity Press, 2012) p.16.
[4]Webster's New World College Dictionary (Cleveland, Ohio: Wiley Publishing, Inc., 2010).

For many Christians, including most ministers and theological students, the Trinity is still a mathematical conundrum, full of imposing philosophical jargon, relegated to an obscure alcove, remote from daily life.[5]

The word trinity is not in the Bible, but the teaching of a three-in-one God is. One example can be seen in the King James Version of John's statement in 1 John 5:7, which reads: "For there are three that bear record in heaven, the Father, the Word, and the Holy Ghost: and these three are one."

The first person of the Trinity is God. God is the Creator and Ruler of the universe. For me, God is Father. I know there are some who have a problem with this paternal concept because of their relationship with their earthly fathers; but for me, as an abandoned child, that is a reason to appreciate God as Father. King David says, "When my father and my mother forsake me, then the Lord will take me up" (Psalm 27:10). This is important to me because as Father, God is an approachable God who longs to have a relationship with His children. Thus, as a child of God, I can experience a relationship with God that is filled with love, intimacy and care.

_____

[5]Robert Letham, *The Holy Trinity in Scripture, History, Theology, and Worship.* (Phillipsburg, NJ: P&R, 2004) p. 1.

The second person of this Trinity is Jesus. Jesus Christ is the Son of God, who is both human and God. In other words, he is God and he is human at the same time. John 1:14 states, "And the Word was made flesh." I take this to mean that God in Jesus became fully human except for sin. He could not have been sinful because then He could not possibly have atoned for sin. Luke 1:1 tells us that Jesus was conceived in the womb of a human mother. Thus, my theological conclusion of this doctrine is that Jesus Christ is the Son of God and is co-equal with God. As a human Jesus lived a sinless life. He died on a cross as a sacrifice for the sins of the world. After three days, He rose from the dead. In this way, Jesus demonstrated his power over sin and death. He ascended to Heaven and someday will return as King of Kings and Lord of Lords. Thus, I further assert that God's ultimate revelation of existence occurred in the incarnation of His Son, Jesus Christ. In John 4:7 we read, "If you had known Me, you would have known My Father also; from now on you know Him and have seen Him."

The scriptures also disclose to us the intimacy within the Trinity. Through the reading of the scriptures, we are taught that God is a God that exists in relationship. In other words, the scriptures imply God as being personal and intimate. John 3:35 tells us, "The Father loves the Son and has placed everything in his hands." This is an important truth because it makes known to us a God we can get close to, talk to and trust. In other words, when we as people accept Jesus, we can talk to a God that hears us. In fact, John 14:13-14 says. "You can ask for anything in my name, and I will do it, because the work of the Son brings glory to the Father. Yes, ask anything in my name, and I will do it." By trusting in the doctrine of the Trinity, we understand God does not exist in isolation. Rather, God is a social God. God, Jesus and the Spirit have always had a close relationship. Moreover, because Jesus prayed that we would be as one even as they are one, I believe we are also created for a relationship with God.

My theological position also speaks of the love of God. Many scripture verses tell us of God's love, but no one of them adequately describes this love in all its facets. John 3:16 describes sacrificial love by saying, "God so loved the world that he gave His only begotten Son." This kind of love is a love I cannot express with words. In fact, it is hard for me to even imagine losing a son at all, but to freely give up a son is doubly hard for me to envision. 1 John 4:10 tells us, "In this is love, not that we loved God, but that He loved us and sent His Son to be the propitiation for our sins." 1 John continues to inform us in chapter 4:12 that "No one has seen God at any time. If we love one another, God lives in us and His love is made complete in us." Here, the word love is used to describe the attraction or the interaction that takes place between God and the people of God.

My theological position speaks of being restored and reconciled to this loving relationship with God, thereby implying that there must have been a separation. Our willingness to disbelieve that God had the best intentions for our lives caused the initial separation of man from God. But God so loved us that God sent Jesus to reconcile humanity to a relationship with God. In theology, the words 'relationship with the Lord' express an idea far beyond my imagination. To think for one moment that the Lord God of the universe finds delight in having a personal relationship with each individual man, woman, boy and girl is outrageous, to say the least. Yet, if God's Word is taken seriously, as written in the Bible, then accepting the loving relationship God offers through Jesus the Christ is essential to life and all related to it. In fact, the overall witness of the Word of God in the Bible is a theological representation of the relationship between God and humanity. It was the death of Jesus that restored this relationship, but it is by the power of the Holy Spirit that this relationship is sealed. Ephesians 4:30 reads, "Do not grieve the Holy Spirit of God, with whom you were sealed for the day of redemption."

The third Person of the Trinity is the Holy Spirit. When Jesus left the earth, we were made a promise that a helper would be sent to us. As difficult as it is to understand the other two natures of Christ, the Holy Spirit is the least understood and the most misinterpreted Person of the Trinity. God the

Holy Spirit is not a "force," nor is the Spirit an "it." The Spirit is a person. The Spirit is also God, co-equal with God the Father and Jesus. The Holy Spirit came to live in the followers of Jesus after Jesus arose from the dead and ascended into heaven. Jesus stated in John 16:7, "Nevertheless I tell you the truth: it is to your advantage that I go away, for if I do not go away, the Advocate will not come to you; but if I go, I will send him to you."

In other words, Jesus is saying if He does not ascend to heaven, then the Spirit will not be sent. I believe that the Holy Spirit works in cooperation with God and Christ in carrying out God's redemptive plan for creation. Jesus goes back, so the Holy Spirit may come to dwell in the hearts of God's people. Hence, the Holy Spirit reveals Jesus to us, and we respond with repentance and faith. Then we ask forgiveness of our sins, and Jesus becomes our Lord and Master. From that moment, the Holy Spirit is present in our lives as a Helper and a Counselor; as a teacher of the Word of God and of how we should pray, as well as a giver of gifts. The Holy Spirit sustains our reconciliation and fellowship with God. Therefore, I believe it is the work of Jesus Christ that reconciled humanity to God, but I also believe that without the power of the Holy Spirit, humanity could not respond to this gift of reconciliation. Paul attests to this point in 1 Corinthians 12:3 when he writes, "No one can say 'Jesus is Lord' except by the Holy Spirit." Thus, my theological position is based on my belief that just as God works above us as the Creator of the universe and just as Jesus Christ works for us as the Redeemer who reconciles us to God; so also, God the Holy Spirit works in us as our Sustainer of life.

Michael Reeves argues that God's purpose in saving humanity is "that the love the Father eternally had for the Son might be in those who believe in him, and that we might enjoy the Son as the Father always has."[6] It is the power of the Holy Spirit that renews our hearts and keeps us mindful of our loving relationship with God. It is through the power of the Cross of Calvary, the death and resurrection of Jesus, and the sending of the Holy Spirit that our personal relationship with God and with one another is restored. Without the Holy Spirit, as humans we would not have the power to glorify Jesus or to recognize ourselves as sinners. It is only by the power of the Holy Spirit that we are led to put our faith in Jesus Christ. Because of the unity the Holy Spirit provides, we not only share the bond between God and Jesus, we also share the community of the Trinity itself in eternity and with all humanity.

---

[6]Michael Reeves, p. 69

Christ and Culture

The reason I chose this project was because of the diversity I meet in my outside ministries. When I am the facilitator for retreats, women's conferences, and revivals, I often find myself ministering to a multi-cultural audience.

The Bible says,
"There is neither Jew nor Greek,
there is neither bond nor free,
there is neither male nor female:
for ye are all one in
Christ Jesus."
Galatians 3:28

While the congregation I preach to each Sunday is predominantly of the Black race and culture, my preaching audience has become more culturally diverse. Continuing with my theological position that through the love of the triune God, people are being restored and reconciled to a relationship with God and each other, I would now like to discuss the issue of Christ and culture.

From the beginning of time, racial, ethical and cultural tensions have always existed among people of faith. The Bible gives us evidence through scripture that Jesus desired cultural reconciliation.

In John 17:21, Jesus prayed for us by saying, "My prayer is not for [the disciples] alone. I pray also for those who will believe in me through their message, that all of them may be one, Father, just as you are in me and I am in you." This verse implies that not only did Jesus come to restore our relationship with God, but also to reconcile our relationship with one another. Jesus modeled a life of racial reconciliation and cultural sensitivity by His association with the Samaritans, the Gentiles, the poor, the sick, women and other outcast people.

Yet, while I believe that Jesus gave us an example of the reconciliation offered to all cultures by both his life and his death, I also believe we still stand in need of unified racial, ethical and cultural restoration and reconciliation. It has taken many followers of Christ decades if not centuries to adjust to this revelation and to put this teaching in action. Overall, I believe we as Christians have failed to exemplify the full potential of reconciliation which Christ came to bring to all cultures. The fact that churches still tend to be quite segregated on Sunday mornings is evidence of the need for reconciliation between believers of all cultures, ethnicities and social statuses throughout America.

My theological position is important to my project because this message of Jesus's death, resurrection and ascension, combined with the power of the Holy Spirit, is preached in most Black pulpits on any given Sunday. The name of Jesus, the blood of Christ, and the cross of Calvary encompass the message of salvation that brings hope to not only the Black culture, but to all who will believe in the works of Jesus from the cross. In Luke-Acts, Luke makes it clear that Paul's preaching is based on Jesus as the Messiah and His work on the cross. In other words, the central theme of Paul's preaching is Jesus Christ, who was crucified and rose from the dead. Paul says in 1 Corinthians 1:18, "The message of the cross seems foolish to those who are lost and dying. But it is God's power to us who are being saved." I like Paul's preaching because it centers on Jesus and what God did through Him on the cross. When I look at the cross and those who were present at the cross, I see evidence that, through what God did on the cross through Jesus, reconciliation was offered to all people no matter their race, gender or social status.

At the Foot of the Cross

As a child coming up, I used to think that the only people at the foot of Jesus's cross when he was crucified were White. I mean after all, that is what we saw in the pictures on the walls, pictures in biblical storybooks, as well as the pictures in my great-grandmother's old Bible on the coffee table. Because all I knew was Black, White and Hispanic, I used to think that at the cross of Jesus one would find people of only one color, one nationality, and one ethnic origin, White. But when I came into the knowledge of Jesus for myself and started to look at the cross of Jesus from a Biblical viewpoint as written in the Word of God, I begin to see that the plurality of ethnicities that make up the family of God is composed of a diversity of races, classes, personalities, and spiritual conditions. There at the foot of the cross was one Simon of Cyrene. According the Gospels recorded by Mark and Matthew, Simon was not only at the cross; he carried the cross for Jesus. Matthew records that "As they went out, they came upon a man from Cyrene named Simon; they compelled this man to carry his cross" (Matthew 27:32 NRSV). Mark records that "They compelled a passer-by, who was coming in from the country, to carry his cross; it was Simon of Cyrene, the father of Alexander and Rufus" (Mark 15:21).

Much debate exists over whether Simon was Black. Research shows that Simon of Cyrene was from a country in ancient northern Africa called Libya. Wikipedia, the online encyclopedia, shares that until recent times, Libya was the home of one the oldest Jewish communities in the world, dating back to at least 300 BC. If we look at this from today's standards, we would have to say that people from North Africa may or may not be classified as Black. But whatever Simon's name implies about his origins, one thing is clear to me personally and that is the fact that Simon of Cyrene was from Ethiopia. People from Ethiopia would undisputedly be classified as Black and that in itself is evidence that all cultures were represented at Calvary's cross.

Also, at the foot of the cross of Jesus were many women who were touched by Jesus in one way or another. Of course, Mary of Nazareth, wife of Joseph the carpenter, mother of Jesus, was standing by the cross. Even though her heart was probably broken, the woman who had carried the very Son of God in her womb and brought Him forth into the world was there. Even though she knew there was nothing she could do to help her son, she stood anticipating the fulfillment of the prophecy that a sword would pierce her soul (Luke 2:35).

While it is possible that she knew that there would be a resurrection after the crucifixion, I am sure she stood there with a pain the magnitude of which only a mother could relate. According to scripture, this pain and sorrow was felt by other women as well. For according to scripture, "Some women were watching from a distance. Among them were Mary Magdalene, Mary the mother of James the younger and of Joseph, and Salome the wife of Zebedee. In Galilee these women had followed him and cared for his needs. Many other women who had come up with him to Jerusalem were also there" (Mark 15:40-41).

Mary Magdalene has often been described as the woman who loved much because she was forgiven much. Some think that before she came to Jesus she was a prostitute, although no written evidence exists to prove that claim. I tend to agree with the viewpoint that she has been confused with one of the many other Mary's mentioned in the New Testament. One clear identifying fact is that scripture reveals her as the woman from whom Jesus cast out seven demons. "After this, Jesus traveled about from one town and village to another, proclaiming the good news of the kingdom of God. The Twelve were with him, and some women who had been cured of evil spirits and diseases: Mary (called Magdalene) from whom seven demons had come out;" (Luke 8:1-2). I contend that it was her gratitude for her deliverance that

[43]

compelled her to follow Jesus not only to the foot of the Cross, but also to the sepulcher to confirm where He was buried.

Scripture also reveals that, on that great resurrection morning, Mary Magdalene was the first to arrive at the open tomb. "Early on the first day of the week, while it was still dark, Mary Magdalene went to the tomb and saw that the stone had been removed from the entrance" (John 20:1). She was also the first to proclaim the news that Jesus had risen from the dead.

> Now Mary stood outside the tomb crying. As she wept, she bent over to look into the tomb 12 and saw two angels in white, seated where Jesus' body had been, one at the head and the other at the foot. They asked her, "Woman, why are you crying? "They have taken my Lord away," she said, "and I don't know where they have put him." At this, she turned around and saw Jesus standing there, but she did not realize that it was Jesus. He asked her, "Woman, why are you crying? Who is it you are looking for?" Thinking he was the gardener, she said, "Sir, if you have carried him away, tell me where you have put him, and I will get him." Jesus said to her, "Mary. "She turned toward him and cried out in Aramaic, "Rabboni!" (which means

"Teacher"). Jesus said, "Do not hold on to me, for I have not yet ascended to the Father. Go instead to my brothers and tell them, 'I am ascending to my Father and your Father, to my God and your God." Mary Magdalene went to the disciples with the news: "I have seen the Lord!" And she told them that he had said these things to her.   (John 20:11-18)

Christianity took on a whole new meaning after the resurrection of Jesus, and who was the first to declare it? None other than a woman named Mary Magdalene.

Among the women mentioned by name who were at the foot of the cross of Jesus was a woman named Salome, the wife of the fisherman Zebedee and mother of James and John. Even though her request for her sons to sit at the right and left of Jesus was denied, she remained a devoted follower of Jesus.

Then the mother of Zebedee's sons came to Jesus with her sons and, kneeling down, asked a favor of him. "What is it you want?" He asked. She said, "Grant that one of these two sons of mine sit at your right and the other at your left." "You don't know what you are asking," Jesus said to them. "Can you drink the cup I am going to drink?" "We can," they answered. Jesus said to them, "You will indeed drink my cup, but to sit at my right or left is not for me to grant. These places belong to those for whom they have been prepared by my Father." (Matthew 20: 20-23)

Salome was also mentioned as one of the women who visited the tomb of Jesus on the morning of his resurrection. "When the Sabbath was over, Mary Magdalene, Mary, the mother of James, and Salome brought spices so that they might go to anoint Jesus' body" (Mark 16:1). The fact that she continued to serve Him even after He was dead indicating that Salome was a woman of great faith and action; a woman who left what could have been a life of comfort and stability in Galilee in order to join her sons as they followed Jesus. Therefore, she was among the privileged women to first learn of Jesus' resurrection. Were these the only women at the cross? No. Mark 15:41 tells us that "Many other women who had come up with him to Jerusalem were also there."

The presence of women at the cross plays a significant role in my theology as well as in this Book, because it serves as additional evidence that women have been redeemed by the promise and fulfillment of Christ's death and resurrection and the power of the Holy Spirit to choose life as a servant of God. We may have started our journey in the Garden of Eden, but our expedition has led us up the hill of Golgotha and on to the empty tomb of Christ, and from there into our hearts comes the message of salvation that says that the ground is level at the foot of the cross. At the foot of the cross, forgiveness is offered to all. Jesus says as he dies on the cross, "Father forgive them for they know not what they do" (Luke 23:34). Through the forgiveness extended to us from the cross and resurrection, life is available to all who will choose to walk in its shadow. In other words, through the love of the triune God, there are no barriers--ethnic, cultural, social, or otherwise--that Christ cannot break through and restore.

Women and Their Restored Authority

For the most part, when the Biblical view on the ministry of women is discussed, only two passages of scripture are referenced, both of which are found in the writings of Paul, in 1 Corinthians and 1 Timothy. Both appear to oppose the idea of women being in leadership positions within the church. I will address these two passages in detail later in this chapter. However, to justify my position on women leadership in the church, I will start with my theological position: Through the love of the triune God, people are being restored and reconciled to a relationship with God and each other.

I would first like to look at the fall of humankind. Genesis 1:26-28 says:

Then God said, "Let us make man in our image, in our likeness, and let them rule over the fish of the sea and the birds of the air, over the livestock, over all the earth, and over all the creatures that move along the ground." So, God created man in his own image, in the image of God he created him; male and female he created them. God blessed them and said to them, "Be fruitful and increase in number; fill the earth and subdue it. Rule over the fish of the sea and the birds of the air and over every living creature that moves on the ground.

It is clear here that God gave the authority to rule over everything to both men and women. However, because today's culture is much different from the cultural in Biblical days, people have different interpretations of scripture as well. With that in mind, a leading question among believers today is the question of what the Bible says about the leadership position of women today. The root of this question comes from the fact that after the fall, the relationship between the man and woman changed. Genesis 3:16 says, "To the woman he said, 'I will make your pains in childbearing very severe; with painful labor you will give birth to children. Your desire will be for your husband, and he will rule over you.'"

Being Black, female and a preacher, I am very aware of this passage of scripture. I am also aware of the fact that there are many interpretations of this passage. Although God never used the word "curse" in this declaration, some call this living in the shadow of the curse of Eve and some call it living in the shadow of males. As for me, I interpret this passage from the perspective of a Black educated female who came up during the era of women's rights in the 1970's. I find that my theology evolves as I grow in my personal experiences as well as in my spiritual academics. My interpretation of this passage is that one of the consequences of Eve's eating the forbidden fruit and of Adam's joining her in this sin was that the woman lost her equality with her husband. The indication here is that God's original plan for equality between the man and woman has changed. For now, instead of the man and woman ruling together, the man was given the authority to rule over his wife. But that was life during that time.

Because I believe that when the sinless man Jesus died on the cross for our sins, the restoration of men and women began immediately; I also believe that at this time the shadow of man's rule over woman was lifted. Consequently, I believe that all women have been redeemed from the past mistakes of Eve and set free to make a choice to follow God's plan for their lives on their own. I think the following New Testament passages of scripture support this argument.

Romans 5:12, 17-19 says,

> Therefore, just as through one-man sin entered the world, and death through sin, and so death spread to all men, because all sinned...For if by the transgression of the one, death reigned through the one, much more those who received the abundance of grace and the gift of righteousness will reign in life through the One, Jesus Christ. So then as through one transgression there resulted condemnation to all men, even so through one act of righteousness there resulted justification of life to all men. For as through the one man's disobedience the many were made sinners, even so through the obedience of the One the many will be made righteous.

1 Corinthians 15:20-22 says,

> But now Christ has been raised from the dead, the first fruits of those who are asleep. For since by a man came death, by a man also came the resurrection of the dead. For as in Adam all die, so also in Christ all shall be made alive.

Galatians 3:25-29 says,

> But now that faith has come, we are no longer under the law. For you are all sons of God through

faith in Christ Jesus. For all of you who were baptized into Christ have clothed yourselves with Christ. There is neither Jew nor Greek, there is neither slave nor free man, there is neither male nor female: for you are all one in Christ Jesus. And if you belong to Christ, then you are Abraham's offspring, heirs according to the promise.

According to this, my theological position leads me to believe that all who are born into the kingdom of God become new creatures in Christ. Therefore, all ethnic distinctions, class separations, and gender differences are abolished and all of God's children who are offered His love, forgiveness, mercy, gifts and grace are restored to equality in Christ Jesus.

I stand on the belief that there was a wide diversity of people at the cross. Blacks were there. People of mixed social and economic backgrounds were there. And, based on this statement in John 12:20-21, "Now there were some Greeks among those who were going up to worship at the feast; these then came to Philip, who was from Bethsaida of Galilee, and began to ask him, saying, 'Sir, we wish to see Jesus'" (John 12:20-21), there may have been some Greeks at the cross. We also know that Roman soldiers, some of whom may have been of Italian descent, were there. This evidence of diversity shows that when Jesus died on that cross, He died for people all over

[51]

the world. In my opinion He died for people of all nationalities, for people of every color, for every ethnic group. On behalf of all of God's children, He died. Thus, this is the group whom I desire to meet with the message of Christ: all who will believe in the resurrection power of God through, Jesus the Christ.

The Power of Pentecost

From the scriptures, it is evident that there was a diversity of people at the cross. The problem is that, in order to gain a hearing with this disparate group of people, one needs more than just the acknowledgment of their presence at the cross. Jesus knew that to get the message of His love out to all people, His disciples would need power from on High. That is why the scriptures say, in Acts 1:4-8, that Jesus:

> Being assembled together with them, he commanded them that they should not depart from Jerusalem, but wait for the promise of the Father, which, saith he, ye have heard of me. For John truly baptized with water; but ye shall be baptized with the Holy Ghost not many days hence. When they therefore were come together, they asked of him, saying, Lord, wilt thou at this time restore again the

kingdom to Israel? And he said unto them, it is not for you to know the times or the seasons, which the Father hath put in his own power. But ye shall receive power, after that the Holy Ghost is come upon you: and ye shall be witnesses unto me both in Jerusalem, and in all Judea, and in Samaria, and unto the uttermost part of the earth.

This power came on the day of Pentecost

When the day of Pentecost came, they were all together in one place. Suddenly a sound like the blowing of a violent wind came from heaven and filled the whole house where they were sitting. They saw what seemed to be tongues of fire that separated and came to rest on each of them. All of them were filled with the Holy Spirit and began to speak in other tongues as the Spirit enabled them

(Acts 2:1-4).

The purpose of Pentecost was to remind the first Christians of their need to do more than just believe and accept the forgiveness granted them at the cross. Rather, in order to do the work, they were commissioned to do, they would need the power of the Holy Spirit.

When the power of the Holy Spirit came upon the disciples, they were able to speak in a diversity of languages. Scripture informs us that at the Tower of Babel, God found it necessary to confuse the languages of the world and to bring about a division among the nations. According Genesis 11: 5-9, at Babel:

> The Lord came down to see the city and the tower the people were building. The Lord said, "If as one people speaking the same language they have begun to do this, then nothing they plan to do will be impossible for them. Come, let us go down and confuse their language so they will not understand each other." So, the Lord scattered them from there over all the earth, and they stopped building the city. That is why it was called Babel because there the Lord confused the language of the whole world. From there the Lord scattered them over the face of the whole earth.

In the plains of Shinar, the people were scattered, and their language was confused to prevent them from trying to make a name for themselves. This confusion of language was reversed in Jerusalem on the day of Pentecost, so that all nations could hear the good news of the Gospel in their own language. The nations were brought together again through the power of the Holy Spirit. Thus, at Pentecost God continued the work of the cross by breaking down the barriers that existed between nationalities, ethnicities, cultures, and races that had been established at the Tower of Babel.

This reinforces my theological position by clearly illustrating that the Gospel is for everybody. It shows that God is not concerned about the color of one's skin. God is not concerned about the race or the social status of neither the one bringing nor the one receiving the Gospel. His plan is for the entire world to hear the message of the Gospel. In order that this may happen, often God's plan calls for agents of God's communication to minister to a people of another race or ethnicity. To do otherwise would be to thwart God's plan.

Another way that the plan of God is thwarted is on the issue of women in ministry. It is not uncommon for preachers who preach liberation to exclude women from that preaching. In fact, many women have had to leave their home churches in search of someone to acknowledge the gift of ministry on their lives. While I can testify to and welcome the changes that are taking place in America today in this field, I can also attest to many instances where preachers and laity are still trying to silence the voice of Black women in the pulpits. That is why my Book seeks to develop strategies to help Black women, as well as women of all ethnicities, to overcome these resistances to hearing the message of the Gospel preached by women.

The fact that God intends to break down the barriers of segregation against gender was reinforced at Pentecost when Peter, quoting the prophet Joel, said:

> And it shall come to pass in the last days, says God, That I will pour out of My Spirit on all flesh; Your sons and your daughters shall prophesy, your young men shall see visions, your old men shall dream dreams. (Acts 2:17)

I do not interpret Peter's use of "prophesy" in this passage to mean to predict the future. In this case, I believe Peter meant "prophesy" to signify the preaching of the good news. Therefore, I am of the assumption that God has called everybody to proclaim the good news, regardless of gender. While today's generation shows some signs of cracks in the barriers of gender discrimination, it is still a struggle for some women to gain a hearing as agents of God called to proclaim the Word of God to all people. This must change. Through the execution of this Book, I hope to develop some strategies that women can employ as an aid to overcoming resistance to their gaining a hearing.

Paul's writings are sometimes misunderstood because the details that led him to write as he did are not clearly known. Craig Keener points out in his book, *Paul, Women, & Wives: Marriage and Women's Ministry in the Letters of Paul,* that there are some inconsistencies in Paul's writings. Keener writes:

> Although many churches would use arguments [from the order of creation] to demand the subordination of women in all cultures, very few accept Paul's arguments [in 1 Cor 11:8–9] as valid for covering women's heads in all cultures. The same argument Paul uses in one passage for forbidding women to teach he uses in another passage to argue that married women . . . must cover their heads in church. In the one passage, Paul does not want the women of a certain congregation to teach; in the other passage, he wants the women of a certain congregation to cover their heads. We take the argument as transculturally applicable in one case, but not so in the other. This seems very strange indeed.[7]

[7]Craig S. Keener, *Paul, Women & Wives: Marriage and Women's Ministry*

Since Paul appears to be contradictory in his writings, rather than just taking his writings literally, we must study the context and the history of them. Some say he writes according to culture. Some say he writes according to the need or the situation. Rebecca Groothuis argues that even this cannot be true. She states:

> If Paul's creation-order rationale here [in 1 Timothy 2:13] renders universal and transcultural the prohibition of women teaching authoritatively, then why doesn't Paul's creation-order rationale for women's head covering (1 Cor. 11:6–9) make the wearing of headgear a universal and transcultural requirement for women in church?"[8]

I don't know what Paul's motives are based on, so personally I try to rely on the Holy Spirit to interpret how I should understand and apply the writings of Paul to my life. Another controversy in Paul's writing can be seen in what John Bristow points out in his book, *What Paul Really Said About Women: An Apostle's Liberating Views on Equality in Marriage, Leadership, and Love,* regarding the number of times that Paul speaks of equality for men and women as

---

in the Letters of Paul, (Peabody, MA: Henderson, 1992) p. 19.
[8]Rebecca Merrill Groothuis, *Good News for Women: A Biblical Picture of Gender Equality*, (Grand Rapids: Baker, 1997) p. 219.

coworkers . To support his argument that Paul supports women, he uses the controversial scripture in which Paul says that women should be silent in church. He points out the fact that Paul did not want disorder in the church, and apparently the women were being disorderly during the worship service. To prevent this disorder, Paul tells the women that they should not speak in church.

When it comes to Scripture, Bristow seems to have the same opinion that I have. He argues that one should strive to understand the overall message of the Gospel even in the face of controversial verses. To prove his point, Bristow looks up the word "silence" in Greek and defines the different meanings of that word. In Bristow's opinion, in this passage Paul uses the Greek word "sigao" when asking the women to be silent. This Greek word in his interpretation means to volunteer.

This implies that Paul is asking the women to voluntarily stop disrupting the worship service. Or in other words, he writes: It is "the kind of silence asked for in the midst of disorder and clamor."[9] As we can see, Paul is often inconsistent in his teachings.

[9]John T. Bristow, *What Paul Really Said About Women: An Apostle's Liberating Views on Equality in Marriage, Leadership, and Love;* (Harper, San Francisco 1988) p.63

Theologian Paul K. Jewett also "understands Paul to be inconsistent with himself regarding the role of women in the church, concluding that Paul advocates sexual equality in one of his books (Gal 3:28) and inequality in another (1 Cor 11:3)."[10] Thus, using the writings of Paul as proof of the subservient roles of women in the church can be very confusing to say the least.

When it comes to Scripture, Bristow seems to have the same opinion that I have. He argues that one should strive to understand the overall message of the Gospel even in the face of controversial verses.

[10]Paul K. Jewett, *Man as Male and Female*; (Grand Rapids, Eerdmans, 1975) p.133-35, 142.

Chapter 2

Theory of Preaching

Introduction

I believe that for one to understand his/her call, there must be a hearing of the call, a discernment of the call, a response to the call, and then a preparation for the ministry of the call. One of my favorite passages of scripture comes from the book of Jeremiah 1:4-5, which says: "The word of the Lord came to me, saying, 'Before I formed you in the womb I knew you, before you were born I set you apart; I appointed you as a prophet to the nations.'" Jeremiah's story begins this way: He said, "The word of the Lord came to me." This informs me that the whole idea of being called to ministry was God's idea, not Jeremiah's. Jeremiah's call had nothing to do with his ambition, his destiny, his skills nor his effort to reach God. He was called by hearing the divine word. Scripture does not reveal whether this word came to Jeremiah by dreams, voices, visual knowledge or feelings. All we know is Jeremiah said, "the word of the Lord came to me."

Like Jeremiah, I, too, was called by the word of the Lord. My story began years ago while I was sitting in the choir stand, looking at the empty pulpit in St. James A.M.E. Church Denton, Texas. I heard God call my name and speak to my heart saying, "Ella, get up and speak." I had heard this voice many times calling my name, but previously had never heard anything called but my name. This time was different. The voice was calling me by name and calling me to action: "Ella, get up and speak." But since I did not know what to say and preferred not to embarrass myself, I chose to just sit there. This call came to me twice in that church in the same way. The second time, I was sitting in the congregation and I did speak, but I said nothing about God because I did not know God at that stage of my life. The next time I heard this voice, it was replaying the scripture reference, "Ephesians 4, Ephesians 4," over and over again in my head while I was sleeping. When I woke up, I got the Bible and read these words:

> As a prisoner for the Lord, then, I urge you to live a life worthy of the calling you have received. Be completely humble and gentle; be patient, bearing with one another in love. Make every effort to keep the unity of the Spirit through the bond of peace. There is one body and one Spirit, just as you were called to one hope when you were called. (Ephesians 4:1-4)

When I next heard this voice, it was saying "1 Corinthians 15:58." Afterwards, I looked up the verse and found this message: "Therefore, my beloved brethren, be ye steadfast, unmovable, always abounding in the work of the Lord, forasmuch as ye know that your labor is not in vain in the Lord." I perceived this to be my original call. It was a call of surrender. God wanted me to serve him; to trust Him by being completely humble and gentle to others; to be patient; to bear others in love; to make an effort to keep the unity of the Body of Christ through the bond of peace. After months of spiritual formation, I responded to God's personal call on my life by saying, "Yes, Lord! Not my will but your will be done" (Matthew 26:39). I then accepted my call and pursued the ordained ministry.

After preaching my preliminary sermon, one of the mothers of the church approached me with these words: "Baby," she said, "everybody is not called." I felt crushed. It was almost enough to make me quit the ministry at the very beginning. That was my first experience with rejection, and it was hard to accept. I shared this experience with Willie Frances McAdams, the lady who had introduced me to Christ. She told me, "You know there are three things against you already. Do you know what they are?" When I looked at her with a confused expression on my face, she told me those three things were race, age and gender. I answered, "I can see where my age and my gender may cause some resistances in my ministry, but I cannot understand how my race affects anything." She said, "Let's just pray that it doesn't."

Thus, from the very beginning of my ministry I was aware of the challenges I had to face as a Black female preacher. But my faith in God's plan for my life as God's agent gave me the strength I needed to pursue my calling, despite the odds that were against me. I kept hearing these words, "Be steadfast, unmovable, always abiding in the works of the Lord for as much as you know your labor in the Lord is not in vain." With these words ringing in my heart, I decided to remain faithful to the call that was on my life. In October 1984, I was ordained an Itinerate Deacon in the African Methodist Episcopal Church. Two years later, in October 1986, I was ordained as Itinerate Elder in the African Methodist Episcopal Church.

When told that I had to do a project for my Doctor of Ministry degree, I thought this would be a good time for me to discover, field test and evaluate some God-given strategies for gaining a hearing. In this chapter of my Book, I will present my theory as to how: (1) my belief in the existence of a loving God, and His Supreme and Ultimate authority over my life; (2) my faith in His Son, Jesus Christ, and what God did through Jesus dying on a cross to forgive my sins, rising from the dead and ascending back to God as my mediator; and (3) my assurance of the power of the Holy Spirit to sustain, protect and empower me to follow God's plan for my life have gained a hearing for me in various cultural contexts. I will also reveal the type of resistances I encountered, as well as what I had to do in order to overcome these resistances.

In my thirty-four years of preaching and pastoring in an African-American cultural context, I have facilitated many conferences and retreats in multi-ethnic settings. When I first began to speak to cultures different from my own, I thought to relate to them, I had to change my approach. Thus, I developed and practiced two unique styles of preaching. When preaching to cultures different from my own, I tended to be more linear and logical in content and delivery. In other words, I prepared messages that had a clear linear connection between the beginning and ending points. Since this was not my normal preaching style, this strategy involved memorizing the message, so I could deliver it in a more dignified and intellectual way. As I look back on that strategy, because I was not being true to myself, this was not the way I should have been presenting the Word of God.

According to the Apostle Paul in his letter to the church in Corinth, the Word of God should be delivered with a demonstration of power of the Holy Spirit:

When I came to you, I did not come with eloquence or human wisdom as I proclaimed to you the testimony about God. For, I resolved to know nothing while I was with you except Jesus Christ and he crucified. I came to you in weakness with great fear and trembling. My message and my preaching were not with wise and persuasive words, but with a demonstration of the Spirit's power, so that your faith might not rest on human wisdom, but on God's power. (1 Corinthians 2:1-5)

By trying to put emphasis on my intellect, I was demonstrating that I was more interested in impressing the congregation with my intelligence than I was in delivering a word from God. I was miserable, and so were they. I was miserable because I was not being true to myself. They were miserable because they were not getting what they expected.

In Chapter 7 of the book, *Beyond Culture,* Edward T. Hall presents his theory of how people communicate based on their cultural differences, using the concepts of high context culture and low context culture.[11] In what he calls a high

---

[11]Edward T. Hall, *Beyond Culture*, (Doubleday Anchor Books, New York

cultural context communication, he states that communicating through relationship and context is more important than communicating through words. Instead of using a lot of words to communicate, people in this context depend more on the speaker's tone of voice, facial expression, gestures and posture for communication. Communication in this context relies on tradition and personal relationships as much as words to impart its message. While Hall does not speak of experiential emotional preaching, what he describes here matches my view of most preaching in my cultural context.

In contrast to high context cultural communication, Hall introduces what he calls a low context cultural communication in which words are the main source of communication. He explains that because this cultural communication relies mostly on the speaker's words, this culture depends more on logical, linear, and action-oriented communication. In other words, listeners want the speaker to communicate expected actions in a candid, concise, and competent way. While Hall does not discuss the conceptual, linear approach to preaching, in my opinion what he describes is the style of most preaching in that cultural context. This Book seeks to answer the question of how these two approaches of communicating the Word of God can be combined to reach various cultures in one setting.

1977) p. 91-131

During a conversation with my D.Min. Advisor, Dr. Alyce McKenzie, she asked me what connection the trinity had to my project. I had just had a conversation with Dr. David Mosser, the Reader for my D.Min. project, about Aristotle's rhetorical persuasions, so I immediately said they are the logos, ethos and pathos of my preaching. At that moment we had a revelation of how those three rhetorical persuasions work together even as a whole in preaching. Just as it takes the trinity to make our lives whole, it takes three rhetorical persuasions to make our message whole. As I thought about that in terms of preaching, I made this connection: logos represent God the Word, pathos represents Jesus the personality of God, and ethos represents the Holy Spirit, the personal passion and conviction of God. In order for preaching to be effective, all three must work together as one.[12] Bryon Chapell writes, "Biblical preaching must consider logos (content), pathos (passion) and ethos (character)."[13] So, I say yes, not only can two approaches to preaching work together to gain a hearing, they must work together.

---

[12]For more on the Aristotelian rhetorical persuasions read: Rhetoric, Logos, Pathos, and Ethos THE THREE "ARTISTIC PROOFS." Henning, Martha L., Friendly Persuasion: Classical Rhetoric--Now! Draft Manuscript. August 1998.

[13]Bryan Chapell, *Christ-Centered Preaching: Redeeming the Expository Sermon* (Baker Press, Grand Rapids, 2005) p. 34

I am an emotional person who likes to express myself emotionally, but I know people need more than emotion to walk with God on this Christian journey. In fact, using Aristotle's rhetorical terms, pathos, logos and ethos, I understand that in order to convince people of their walk with God, not only their emotions, but also their character and their mind must be stirred. I am not using my emotions in an attempt to stir the emotions of the listeners in hopes of creating some desired emotional response. This kind of emotional excitement can give people a brief pleasure, but pleasure cannot change their lives or the circumstances of their lives. No, for people to have a life-changing experience, they need to have a spiritual encounter with God that can only come through the persons of God, Jesus and the Holy Spirit working in their lives.

This informs me that the presence of God is not something that can be obtained by the preacher stirring up emotions. The presence of God does not show up because there is singing and praying in a worship service. The presence of God is only promised to come when we are in one accord and together in the name of Jesus. When I say emotional, I speak of my response to an experience with God that made a difference in my life.

When I think of Jesus and all He has done for me, my emotions are stirred, and I do not mind expressing it. Thus, I find the best way to present the Word of God to the people of God is to just simply be myself. In other words, I have learned when delivering God's message in various cultural contexts, it is not my style of preaching that needs to be adjusted, but rather it is my awareness of to whom I am preaching that needs adjusting. I do not need to become more dignified to gain a hearing. What I need is to become more aware of the hearers' culture, so that I might customize the message to accommodate their needs logically, emotionally and characteristically.

Worship in the Black Church

In the book, *African-American Christian Worship*, Melva Wilson Costen gives her readers an explanation of the historical and theological beginnings of the African-American worship tradition. As she explains how music, preaching, and prayer have shaped the African American worship, I am convinced that the spiritual basis of our preaching is all about finding God in the struggles of life. Costen explains the connection between the practice of worship and the influence it has on the rest of life. She writes "In order for corporate worship to be authentic and empowering, it must be psychologically relevant to worshipers and commensurate with their lived experience."[14] In making this connection between worship, faith, and hope, as practiced in the lives of African Americans, Costen implies that whether or not some African Americans see God at all is sometimes based on whether or not they see God in the everyday struggles of life.

Thus, in most African American churches, the focus of worship is more on the knowledge of what God has done and can do to help with the concerns and problems faced in society than on the theology about the existence and nature of God. Therefore, culturally all my worship experience has been built around a highly emotional setting, where one uses singing, dancing, shouting, hand clapping, and the preaching of God's Word to freely express his or her excitement about the assurance of God's grace. In fact, for many, the hymn "Blessed Assurance Jesus Is Mine," stands as the foundation of their worship and the place of their passion. Every time I sing "This is my story, this is my song, praising my Savior all the day long," I get excited about both who I am and whose I am! These words of the assurance of God's grace say to me, I may be desperately struggling to make sense of my life, but one thing I know for sure is, because of the resurrection of Christ, I too have life now and eternally. Dr. Alyce McKenzie in answering the question, "Why I need the Resurrection," blogged this response:

---

[14]Melva Wilson Costen, *African-American Christian Worship* (Abingdon Press, Nashville 1st edition 1993) p. 123

Without the Resurrection I would strongly suspect that living for others, despite the cost, brings life. But how would I know for sure? With the knowledge that Jesus Christ, who was crucified, is yet alive, my suspicion is confirmed. I need the Resurrection so that I won't spend my life waiting until it's too late to live for him, which means to live for others. The Resurrection prevents my being like Joseph of Arimathea who tenderly cared for the body of Jesus, but only after he was dead. It empowers me to care for Jesus' body, knowing that he lives![15]

Amen, Dr. McKenzie! Yes, He does. My Savior lives. Another favorite hymn of the church, "Because He Lives" written by Bill and Gloria Gaither say it well through these lyrics:

> God sent his son, they called Him Jesus He came to love, heal and forgive, He bled and died to buy my pardon an empty grave is there to prove my Savior lives. Chorus - Because He lives, I can face tomorrow Because He lives, all fear is gone. Because I know, He holds the future. And life is worth the living just because He lives.

[15]Dr. Alyce McKenzie, (blog at http://www.patheos.com/Resources/Additional-Resources/Why-I-Need-the-Resurrection.html)

Because I believe this, it is my desire to preach the cross and resurrection of Christ with my heart, my soul, and my mind. Costen further asserts that "African people tend to seek to know God personally rather than to know about God from doctrines and creeds."[16] In the African Americans' worship experience, most expect to leave their places of worship with a renewed hope that will help them cope with joblessness, poverty, discrimination and oppression. The African American slaves made worship a part of their everyday living. In spite of the fact that this "liberating" Gospel was introduced to them by their oppressor, they kept their faith in an unseen God and continued to worship God in what Costen calls an "Invisible Institution."

According to Costen, "All African American denominations (Protestant especially) can claim heritage in the Invisible Institution, regardless of when and where they enter denominational history."[17] Because of this, their hope was restored, and communities of faith, belief systems and practices were formed. Faith and hope are historically essential to all African American worship. I can attest to the fact that faith is a very important part of our spiritual existence. In fact, faith is the reason many of us go to church each Sunday. On our best day, it is our faith in Christ that dictates how we interact with

---

[16] Ibid, p.20
[17]Ibid. p. 87

one another and the world. It is faith in Jesus that assures us that all God's children can live in peace with one another, no matter what the race, ethnicity, gender or creed of our brothers and sisters.

Costen goes on to say, "The most effective demonstration of true liturgy is what we do in obedience to God in Christ with our lives when we gather and when we scatter as a community in the world."[18] Thus, in worship, true liturgy brings about liberation in three ways: empowerment, hope and victory. When the Holy Spirit appears, and people participate in the worship experience, everyone shares an appreciation and affirmation that through the power and presence of God's Holy Spirit healing, transformation and victory are taking place in the lives of God's people. African American worship aims at bringing about self-worth, self-esteem and self-value in the lives of people who feel robbed of all that is virtuous and appropriate. It is because of hope in the life, death and resurrection of Jesus that many Blacks have accepted the fact we are the work of the hand of God who created a "marvelous work," hence, we are "fearfully and wonderfully made." (Psalms 139:14)

Preaching in the Black Church

---

[18]Ibid. p.127

The history of African American preaching began as far back as the days of slavery in America. Because it was illegal for a slave to learn to read or write, they developed a verbal method of reaching the spiritual needs of the society. This was done through passing the message of God down to each generation though the oral practice of singing spiritual songs, telling folk tales and preaching sermons. Although the slave preachers could not read the Bible, they knew the Bible stories. In their own creative way, they used those stories to help the slaves survive their oppression by assuring them that God was on their side and they would be free one day. Thus, the Black church became the center of freedom of the Black race. It was the only place where Blacks felt safe to gather and share their common anxieties as a free society of faith. It was the only place where Blacks could stand independent and free.

Costen writes:

> In true and authentic worship of God there
> is a dialectical relationship rather than a
> dichotomy between faith and practice,
> justice and ritual action, (liturgy and
> justice) theological talk and doxological
> living, and sanctification and human
> liberation.[19]

---

[19]Ibid. p. 126

In other words, because personal experience is an important spiritual element of worship in most Black churches, worship involves more than merely performing rituals.

C. F. Stewart asserts that Black preaching in any context is "one of the most powerful idioms of freedom for Black people in America."[20] Freedom distinguishes the story that shapes the style and theology of Black preaching. Long before Blacks were allowed into politics or to have any governmental rights at all, there was the Black church and the Black preacher. I honestly believe that without the Black church and the Black preacher, Blacks in America may have given up hope of ever seeing freedom. The name of the church of which I am a member, the African Methodist Episcopal Church, was originally the Free African Society. Its sister church, the African Methodist Episcopal Zion Church, was called Freedom Church.

It is my opinion that these churches use the name "Freedom" because it was the Black church that took on the task of protecting African Americans from the injustice that they experienced. I believe that if it had not been for the Black church and the Black preacher during their greatest hour of oppression, all hope would have been lost for this race of

---

[20]C. F. Stewart, *Soul Survivors: An African American Spirituality* (Louisville, KY: Westminster John Knox Press, 1997) p. 146.

people. But God had a ram in the bush that fanned the fire of freedom in the hearts of the Black race.

When discrimination, segregation and oppression made Blacks in American feel degraded and dehumanized, it was the Black preacher behind the voice that moved them to freedom. They may not have been able to read or write, but they could sing. So, the Black church and the Black preacher kept Blacks in America unified and educated; and the unique way in which they did this was through singing the message that they wanted the people to know. To some people these were just songs, but according to my great-grandmother, Bernice Anderson, during the times when Blacks felt dishonored and it seemed that no one cared about their conditions, they would go to the church where the Black preacher would preach and lead them in singing songs like, "We Are Our Heavenly Father's Children," and "We All Know that He Loves Us, One and All."

I believe that if it had not been for the Black church and the Black preacher during their greatest hour of oppression, all hope would have been lost for this race of people.

When Black females were robbed of their dignity and their hope and Black males were worn and weary both physically and spiritually, the Black preacher helped them to hold on until their change came by leading them in singing songs like, "Walk Together Children, Don't Get Weary." And when the light of life started to get dim, it was the Black preacher who told the people "over yonder, you will sit at a welcoming table; you will eat and never hunger, drink and never get thirsty!" These songs were really sermons, and they delivered messages of hope for freedom.

Theologically, freedom is still a major emphasis in the Black church, and the Black preacher still has the responsibility today to move the church towards it. The difference is instead of freedom through singing, we must now lead people to freedom through reading the Word of God. The Black preacher's charge is to see to it that the church remains true to the Gospel of Jesus Christ. The Gospel tells us about a different kind of freedom, a freedom that comes from accepting Jesus Christ into your heart; a freedom that comes from knowing the truth will truly set your heart free; a freedom that has eternal implications.

This is the type of preaching that shapes the style and theology of Black preaching today.

According to Bishop Vashti Murphy McKenzie in <u>Those Sisters Can Preach! 22 Pearls of Wisdom, Virtue and Hope</u>:

> The black preacher must bring the totality of herself or himself to the message; the message cannot become about the preacher, for then it will veer from the biblical mandate to preach the gospel. The message must be biblically based and rooted in the preacher's relationship with God and the preacher's connection with the Holy Spirit. The message must both encourage us and call us to accountability.[21]

Worship then becomes a celebration through which African Americans are empowered by the preached word to go forth and share the good news of Jesus Christ with others. Costen asserts that worship empowers the worshiper to provide acts of service to others, and to establish relationships that are built on "oneness in Christ Jesus."[22]

Bishop McKenzie writes: "Preaching is the divine encounter between God, the preacher, and those who would

---

[21]Vashti Murphy McKenzie, *Those Sisters Can Preach!; 22 Pearls of Wisdom, Virtue and Hope*, (The Pilgrim Press, Cleveland, Ohio 2013) p. vii
[22]Costen Ibid. 126

hear God's proclaimed Word."[23] Often when we think of having a divine encounter with God, we think of the encounters that people like Abraham, Moses, and Jeremiah had. After Abraham's encounter with God, he left his homeland, his family and his friends and traveled to an unidentified land among strange people. Moses' encounter with God sent him back home to face the people away from whom he ran. After Jeremiah had his encounter with God, he became the only visible light of truth in a time of severe darkness. But when I look at these people, I do not see where their encounter with God brought about a change in their relationship with God and others. What changed in each of these instances was the direction of their lives. Each of these men witnessed the power of God in miraculous ways.

The children of Israel also witnessed such miracles, but they responded by complaining, doubting, and rebelling against God. Although they were obedient about doing what God called them to do, they did not allow their encounters to change their lives. While it is important to be obedient to the call of God, we must also respond to that call with faith, trust and love. It is almost impossible for persons proclaiming faith in God to gain a hearing with others, if that faith is not demonstrated.

------

[23]McKenzie ibid

[80]

I believe that's why Bishop McKenzie continues by saying, "In order for authentic preaching to occur, the preacher must have a transforming relationship with God, about whom she or he speaks."[24] I believe the relationship of which she speaks is one of trust, faith, and love. This is the relationship that must exist between God, the preaching, and the people who hear the Word of God proclaimed to them. In other words, Bishop Vashti McKenzie is implying that authentic preaching should address the mind, engage the heart and confront the conscience of the hearers. When one has had this type of spiritual encounter with God, it should result in a spiritual rebirth that by the indwelling of God's Holy Spirit empowers believers to resist sin and to become more Christ-like in their daily living.

So, when experiential preaching has taken place, a saving faith in Christ should transform their relationships with God and others, when applied to the believers' mind, heart and will. Paul says in Romans 12:2, we should be transformed by the renewing of our minds. Therefore, for those who preach the Word of God, if we wish to gain a hearing from those to whom we preach, there must not be only a change in the direction of our lives, but there must also be a change in our ways of thinking and the manner in which we align our lives with the

---

[24]Ibid.,

truth (*logos*, the content and ideas of a message) of God's Word. The preached word should move (*pathos,* the feelings generated by the sermon) those who preach it and those who hear it to seek to live moral and spiritual lives (*ethos,* the character of the preacher). Bishop McKenzie continues with this statement: "In the African American context, preaching has been considered as both a folk and a fine art; hence, it cannot simply be viewed as communication alone."[25] Said another way, preaching in the African American culture involves the use of more than words. Bishop McKenzie continues, "For in the African American pulpit, there are unique expectations of the Black preacher, which are different from those in other cultural contexts."[26]

Robert Franklin, President of ITT, explains it this way:

> Black Christians have come to expect sermons to be poetic masterpieces that are biblically rooted, politically prophetic, intellectually stimulating, emotionally evocative, rhetorically polished, pastorally positive, personally sensitive, and reverently and joyfully delivered. [27]

---

[25]Vashti Murphy McKenzie, p. vii.
[26]Ibid.,
[27]Black Homiletic: (http://www.preachersmagazine.org/articles/36-sermons/873-black-homiletic-a-unique-experience-on-the-preaching-landscape).

One method of this style of preaching can be experienced in what the Black church calls "the whoop." Because I have much experience in this area of preaching, I know firsthand that, if done right, this can be a very emotional experience for both the preacher and the listeners in most Black cultural contexts. By definition, the whoop is a preaching style of delivery that some preachers use at the close of their sermon message. While the whoop is very popular and often expected sermonic strategy in the Black church, it is not unique to Black churches only. It is used by other cultures as well. This technique calls for the preacher's voice to change from the normal tone to a musical tone while the preacher makes the closing summary at the end of the preaching event.

Often, in the Black tradition when the question is asked, "Can the preacher preach?" they are really asking, "Can the preacher whoop?"

Whooping is often combined with a method of preaching called "call and response." I will write more about this later in the book. Good whoopers are theologically sound preachers who can tell the story with a great passion for the Word of God. When I say, "done right," I refer to the difference between whooping and yelling. Some Black preachers give neither thought nor preparation to the conclusion of their sermon. They think they can just take it to the cross and whoop their way out. However, what they end up doing is simply yelling. The whoop is not just something that comes at the end of the sermon. It should be adequately prepared. Personally, I like the emotional experience associated with the whoop. Nevertheless, I believe the preacher should have something to celebrate before moving into the whooping stage!

Theoretically, I believe preaching should have as its main focus the leading of individuals into deciding to accept and to live for Christ. Secondly, I believe good preaching should encourage individuals to grow spiritually by studying the Bible. And, thirdly, I believe good preaching should convict individuals of their sinfulness, so they may repent and be saved. This is the root of Christ-centered experiential preaching which convicts sinners of a saving faith through a personal encounter with God. If the sermon has done these things, then there is reason to celebrate! This works well in my worship setting as a Black preacher, but I wonder how well this theory transfers across cultures? This is one question I will explore in this Book.

Christ-Centered Preaching

Preaching Christ-centered messages sometimes directly involves an intensive doctrinal study of the scriptures. Yet, in many cases, it discloses how Christ is revealed in the solution to the condition of humankind. Bryan Chapell says, "Christ-centered preaching rightly understood does not seek to discover where Christ is mentioned in every text but to disclose where every text stands in relation to Christ"[28] This kind of preaching requires one to have a faith that is centered in the grace of Christ. This assurance of grace can only come from the power of God through the preaching of the cross and resurrection of Jesus Christ. If this Word of God is preached and heard, my faith leads me to believe that God will not withhold access to this grace from anyone who will accept it through Jesus Christ. In other words, because the assurance of grace through Jesus Christ is secure, all people have free access to the grace of God.

Christ-centered preaching is essential to my Book because I truly believe that Christ, the crucifixion and resurrection, are the only message of salvation. This is the message I believe preachers must proclaim. The problem is that not all who hear the preaching of cross and resurrection are convinced that it is the only means by which salvation is obtained. Many are looking for another. It used to be that the preaching of the cross and resurrection of Jesus was enough to convince reasonable thinking people of salvation, through

---

[28]Chapell Ibid., p. 279

accepting what God did through Jesus by way of the cross and resurrection. But, I find in many of today's cultures, such preaching has been replaced by practical superficial motivational preaching. People want to hear messages today that tell them how to become successful and how to have better lives. Because many people have come to expect these kinds of messages, when the cross and resurrection are preached they tune the preacher out.

According to Bryan Chapell, the "Bible is not a self-help book. The Scriptures present one, consistent, organic message. They tell us how we must seek Christ who alone is our Savior and source of strength to be and do what God requires." [29] He further warns that any messages that are "not Christ-centered or redemptive focused become human-centered messages."[30] These messages, he implies, have a focus on the "deadly Bs."[31] Further, he warns that these messages fall under the category of "Be Like Messages,"[32] which encourage the listeners to be like a particular biblical personality. Then there are the "Be Good Messages,"[33] which imply that by applying a right behavior the believers can secure a relationship with God on their own. Finally, he points to what he calls "Be

---

[29]Ibid. 287
[30]Ibid. 289
[31]Ibid.,
[32]Ibid.,
[33]Ibid.,

Disciplined Messages" [34] that stress the believer can have a better relationship with God if they put forth an improved effort to improve themselves. According to Chapell, all of these "Be Messages" are deadly because they assume we can bypass the saving work of Christ and can do something ourselves to correct our fallen condition.

I believe another reason some Black preachers fail to gain a hearing when preaching the Gospel of Jesus Christ in various cultural contexts is because they focus too much on their cultural oppressions. African Americans who were born before the seventies have a very vivid memory of such things as slavery, separate but equal doctrine, Jim Crow laws, segregated schools, and poll tax voting laws. The only place African Americans had to go for a relief from these oppressions was the Black church. It was at the Black church where they heard messages that suggested because of Jesus' death on the cross and his resurrection from the dead, a day was coming when they too would overcome their oppression. So, the message of the cross became the message of hope for social justice and social action. Back then, people trusted God to redeem them through the cross of Christ. Scripture references such as: "Vengeance is mine says the Lord," and

---

[34]Ibid.,

"They that wait on the Lord shall renew their strength" were seen as words of assurance in most Black worship settings.

Regrettably, as time passed the message of the cross and resurrection in many Black churches was replaced with messages of hope for other social issues. In other words, some "controversial issues on which Christians disagree"[35] sometimes cast a shadow on the message of the cross, which in some cases was banned as a message of hope because it was seen as too bloody. The problem with this is that rather than the Gospel being used to gain a hearing for Christ during these circumstances, concerns over such issues were ranked above the message of the cross and resurrection. The result of this change in focus is that some are persuaded to accept the message of Christ as a way to remain in their sin rather than to be saved from their sin. As Dr. Alyce McKenzie states: "There is a difference between using scripture (and preaching) to support the preacher's stand on a hotly debated issue, and focusing sermons on the love of God as shown to us in Jesus' life, death, resurrection and ongoing presence."[36]

In other words, because certain social issues and circumstances do not cross all cultural lines, preaching on these circumstances will not change a person's life or turn a soul

_____

[35]Alyce McKenzie, Teacher to Student Advisor notes, 3-5-2014
[36]Ibid.

toward God. In such cases as this, what usually happens is the preacher ends up using the name of Jesus as a tactic to make people feel better about themselves, their situations and their circumstances. This kind of preaching in my opinion only uses Jesus as a means of convincing people that their problems are solved. This result will not last long, for as soon as these individuals begin to feel bad or to live bad lives again, they will turn from Jesus with distrust. In order for conversion to take place, for lives to be changed, for circumstances to be turned around, our message must be Christ-centered.

Thus, in order to overcome the resistance to gaining a hearing of the message of salvation, the preacher must return to preaching Christ-centered messages. Only then will the messages of the cross and resurrection be heard across cultures. Fr. James Feehan writes:

> If the pulpit is not committed to this utter centrality of the Cross, then our preaching, however, brilliant, is doomed to sterility and failure. We preach the Christ of the Mount; we preach the Christ of the healing ministry; we preach the Christ of the sublime example; we preach the Christ of the Social Gospel; we preach the Christ of the Resurrection but rarely, if ever, do we preach the Christ of the Cross. We have

evaded the very heart of the Christian message. In our preaching we tend to decry the human predicament, the turmoil of our lives, the evil in the world, and we wonder if there is a way out. The Way Out is staring us in the face. It is the Way of Christ, the Way of the Cross.[37]

If we are to preach messages that save, we as preachers must again turn to the preaching of the cross and resurrection. Otherwise, we may end up preaching everything, but Christ crucified on the cross and risen from the grave. This is the topic which one must seek to preach if he/she expects to gain a hearing in various cultural contexts.

The good news of the Gospel is that, to gain a hearing, it does not need any skills other than the preaching of the cross and resurrection. However, the problem with the preaching of the cross is that it is rarely preached in a manner that is relevant to the daily needs of humankind, and thus too often falls on deaf ears. What is needed in the church today is a preaching of the Gospel message in such a way that it is obvious Christ came to save everyone. The message of the cross and resurrection is a message of forgiveness, reconciliation, and love. Through the acceptance of this message, all cultures have access to the grace of God given through the life, death and

[37]Fr. James Feehan, *Preaching Christ Crucified: Our Guilty Silence* (The Mercier Press, Dublin Irland, 1991) p.19.

resurrection of Jesus Christ. So, if the Black female preacher desires to gain a hearing in various cultural contexts, she must not rely on social ethics, stories of success, or tactics of overcoming as her method of gaining a hearing. The only way to gain a hearing is to correctly teach the word of truth about Jesus and the power of the cross and resurrection.

The purpose of Christ-centered messages as preached by Paul in Luke-Acts was to cause his listeners to make a decision about Christ, as with the jailer in Acts 16:31 who asked, "What must I do to be saved?" What this says to me as it relates to my Book is that preaching should do more than offer the congregation a reflection; it should stir up an emotional movement that brings about a change in the emotional, the volitional, the intellectual and the spiritual aspects of the hearer's life. Bishop Vashti Murphy McKenzie writes,

> "There is no room in the contemporary African American pulpit for vacuous preaching; preaching that neither effectively proclaims the message of the gospel nor significantly engages the hearer."[38] In other words, Bishop McKenzie is implying how what we as preachers say is critical, but it only becomes critical if we have

---

[38]Vashti Murphy McKenzie, Ibid., p. vii

something to say. What this says to me as it relates to this Book is that the preaching of the Word should do more than offer the congregation a reflection; it should touch the heart, mind and soul of the believer, creating a persuasion that makes a way for Christ to transform and bring about a change in the lives of the hearers.

It is the assurance of the forgiveness and salvation of the cross and resurrection of Christ that provides the emotional and motivational force behind most preaching in my culture. Since I believe preaching should be Christ-centered and challenging, this preaching project is inspired by my desire to preach Christ-centered messages that can be heard in any cultural context with the power and authority given to me as an agent of God's communication.

It is also my desire to pastor a multi-cultural church, therefore I need to develop preaching strategies that will be culturally friendly. Finally, it is my desire to develop preaching strategies that will encourage Black female preachers to boldly stand their ground and be who they are when preaching beyond their own cultural context and worship setting. It is my prayer that this Book will provide some valuable preaching strategies that can be utilized as resources to assist Black female preachers who are called to step out of the box and to minister in diverse cultures. Thus, in order to overcome the resistance to gaining a hearing of the message of salvation, the preacher must return to preaching Christ-centered messages. Only then will the messages of the cross and resurrection be heard across cultures.

Chapter 3

Project Report-The Design

Introduction

This Project is designed to determine whether the experiences of a Black female preacher, who has been for the most part successful in ministering in various cultural contexts, can be used to develop sermonic strategies that can be applied by other Black female preachers as an aid to overcoming the resistances they may encounter to gaining a hearing in various cultural contexts.

In March 2012, I was asked by a large church, having at least 95% Caucasian membership, to facilitate their first women's retreat. The individual who invited me had attended a women's retreat at another church for five consecutive years, for which I had been the facilitator. When her church became interested in having a women's retreat, she recommended that I become the facilitator and her suggestion was accepted by the church. Somehow an associate pastor of that church, who was also a female minister, became involved in the planning of the retreat. At that point, it was suggested that I allow this associate pastor to send me an outline of the messages they wanted presented at the retreat.

Because I had worked many Emmaus Walks in which there is an outline that must be followed for each presenter, I agreed to this procedure. I thought this would be an easy task, until I received the outline and began working on the messages. I found what was supposed to be an outline was more of a manuscript. The more I worked on the message, the more confused I became as to the purpose of this request. While everything about me was saying, "Don't do it," because I had already agreed to be the facilitator and agreed to accept the outline, I felt compelled to honor my commitment.

In my frustration, I tried to make a connection between this request and the Emmaus Walk, in which the purpose of the outlines is to ensure that each participant on a Walk is presented with the same basic information as participants on other Emmaus Walks. I am familiar with and understand this, since the order of worship in the African Methodist Episcopal Church was designed so church goers would be familiar to it and, thereby, feel at home and comfortable no matter what African Methodist Episcopal Church they attended. However, there was no connecting relationship between those situations and this church's women's retreat.

Despite my uncertainties, I prepared the messages that I was to present by following the outline almost word for word as it was suggested. As a result, while I was presenting the messages, I found myself making disclaimer remarks before each statement, such as, "I am supposed to say," or "It is suggested that I tell you." I had prepared someone else's ideas, and I was not comfortable presenting them as my own. This was not who I was, and I did not feel comfortable making the presentations, nor did I feel free to follow the promptings of the Holy Spirit. Thus, I found myself in an awkward predicament from which I did not know how to gracefully escape.

Finally, after the second message or so, the associate pastor came to me and said, "You do not have to say anymore that you are 'supposed to say,' or that you 'have been told to say.' Just forget the outline and present the message you want to present." I thanked her, went back to my room and re-wrote the remainder of the presentation using some experience, examples, testimonies and ideas that I had about the topic. During the next presentation, I felt the power of God's Holy Spirit come in and move me to a new level of facilitating. It felt so good to be able to depend on God and His Holy Spirit to minister and speak through me. Being set free from trying to please people, I was freed to witness to what I had heard the Spirit speaking to me about the Word of God. That is what preaching is all about. It is speaking about what the preacher has heard God speak, not what the preacher is told by another human to speak. The authority given to the preacher to preach is not based on the preacher's perception, title, or influence; rather, it is based upon what that preacher has experienced, heard or seen in the scriptures through illumination or the power of God's Holy Spirit.

In his book, *The Witness of Preaching*, Thomas Long says, "The preacher as witness is not authoritative because of rank or power but rather because of what the preacher has seen and heard."[39] So, in my opinion, in order to authentically witness to the Word of God, the preacher must be free to study and listen to the scriptures as interpreted by the Holy Spirit. Then and only then can the preacher testify as to what he or she has heard God say. If a preacher is to testify to what the Lord says, he or she must first have heard, listened, and trusted the Holy Spirit to speak through him or her, no matter the cultural context in which he or she speaks. Because I was deprived of this freedom in the first presentations at that retreat, no hearing of the Word of God was taking place in those first messages. Because I could not hear God speaking to me, the women could not receive a word from God through me. But, once the Spirit had set me free, the atmosphere changed.

---

[39]Thomas G. Long, *The Witness of Preaching*, (Louisville, KY: Westminster John Knox Press, 2005), 47.

The associate pastor later came and asked me if I knew why she had given me the outline. I responded, "I guess you had to." She responded, "No, I did not have to." I ended the conversation at that point out of fear of being insulted. In other words, I chose to bypass this resistance to gaining a hearing by avoiding any possible insult to my character and/or intelligence. Furthermore, no matter what she said after that, I realized it was I who had allowed Christ to be removed from the center of my motivation for preaching. It was I who had listened and given someone other than the Holy Spirit the authority to speak through me. From this experience I determined never again to divert from trusting the leading of the Holy Spirit.

The Planning Stages of this Project had Seven Steps

The first step was to get my local congregation to support the project. Since the majority of the work for this project was to be done away from the local church setting, I needed them to give me the necessary freedom to work on it. I also needed them to participate in hosting two of these diverse worship services. Likewise, I needed at this time to select and confirm the venues of the preaching engagements.

The second step of this Project was to write the evaluation questionnaire, so I made an appointment with my field supervisor to discuss the project with her. We met at

Pappadeaux Seafood Restaurant in Duncanville, Texas and discussed the project over lunch. During this meeting, we also spoke about the design of the evaluation form. I used her suggestions, along with my ideas and the expertise of my advisory teacher, to design a written evaluation questionnaire that would be used to evaluate the sermons I preached as part of this project. The evaluation form was objective and subjective. It asked for the name, culture, and age of the evaluator. The questionnaire evaluated the theological and Biblical claim of the sermon; the connectedness of the sermon to the cultural context of the hearers; the sermonic focus, function and form of the sermon; the usefulness of the illustrations and stories used in the sermon; a section for the constructive feedback on the delivery, presence and helpfulness of the sermon; and a space for personal opinions about the sermon. Examples of the letter, the blank questionnaire and the completed questionnaire are included in the appendices of this report.

After receiving approval of the evaluation form from my field supervisor and my advisor, I was encouraged to proceed with **the third step** of the Project, which was to plan and confirm the preaching opportunities. I needed to preach in four diverse cultural contextual settings. I planned to preach to a diverse congregation, a Black congregation, a White congregation, an Asian congregation and a Hispanic congregation. However, I could not find an Asian pastor that would allow me to address the congregation. Once these engagements were confirmed, **the fourth step** was to seek a scriptural text that could be used to preach a message that would be Christ-centered and theologically sound, as well as logical and emotional, to be accepted in any cultural context.

The **fifth step** was to select six clergy women who would volunteer to be a part of an advisory team. Their responsibilities were to help with the evaluation of the Project, to give their thoughts on the process, sermons and interviews, and to help compile facts and draw conclusions about the Project. I could not get six clergy women, so I recruited two clergy and four lay persons to help with this step. I chose three Black women and three White women who would observe my preaching in my cultural context as well as in various other settings. Their written evaluations are included in the appendix of this book.

The **sixth step** was to choose three Black female pastors of congregations outside their own culture who would agree to help me with my Project by allowing me to interview them. I met with these three women twice. The first meeting was a get-acquainted session. The second meeting was the actual interview session. In this session, each pastor was asked about the resistances they face and what they had learned from the resistances. Depending on their answers, in some cases there were further follow up questions asked for the purpose of clarity and more information.

As a final test of these sermonic strategies, **the seventh step** was to invite another Black female preacher to preach in a unified diverse setting. I invited my friends from all cultures, denominations and races to attend. I borrowed a sanctuary for the occasion. I will say more about this engagement later in The Project Report Chapter and again in the Critical Evaluation Chapter of this Book.

This Book was designed to give both the proclaimers of the Word and hearers of the preached word of God a chance to observe and evaluate sermonic strategies that may be used to overcome the resistance to gaining a hearing of the Word of God preached by a Black female preacher sharing a Christ-centered message. The Project evaluation form critiqued sermonic strategies used to present the message. It is my hope that strategies may be developed from this Project that other Black female preachers may benefit from when facing resistance to gaining a hearing and when preaching a challenging message both in and beyond their cultural context. If a preacher is to testify to what the Lord says, he or she must first have heard, listened, and trusted the Holy Spirit to speak through him or her not matter the cultural context.

Chapter 4

The Project Report; The Practicum

Introduction

When I started the D. Min course of study in January 2010, I was recovering from a major setback in my ministry. In May 2009, I had been assigned by the Bishop of the AME Church to become the pastor of the second largest church in my district. The church heard about my appointment and immediately began to protest, not because of my preaching but because I am a female. Many of them had heard me preach, but none of them knew me. They liked my preaching, but they did not want a female pastor, and they were going to make sure they did not get one. The things they said about me were so painful that I almost lost focus on who I was as an agent of God. I had a very successful ministry with an outstanding record, which included some great achievements. Hence, I could not understand how they could make up such vicious lies and spread such character assassinations about me. Up until this point, I was very naive about the resistance women faced in ministry. However, this experience made me aware that the resistance was real, and I was not exempt.

Even though I did not plan to continue the D. Min course of study after that first semester, because I had enrolled and had been accepted in the program, I decided to give the first class a try. I knew both instructors, Dr. Alyce McKenzie and Dr. Elaine Heath. Both were also female preachers and had been my teachers before in the M. Div. program; therefore, I felt comfortable taking this class. It was Dr. McKenzie who took notice of the change in my character. She remembered the enthusiasm and joy I once showed in the past and was curious as to what had happened to it. So, she made an appointment with me in hopes of helping me regain that demeanor. Talking to her did help me to regain my focus. The pain of the experience was still there, but she helped me face that resistance by reminding me that who I am in Christ does not change because of other peoples' insinuations and accusations. Because of my meeting with Dr. Alyce McKenzie, I felt I had a connection with her, so I chose her as my project advisor. She helped me to understand the resistance women face in ministry, and I believed she could help me stay focused on this project. With Dr. McKenzie's help, my topic for this project was simplified to this theme, *Black, Female and a Preacher: Sermonic Strategies for Overcoming the Resistances to Gaining a Hearing in Various Culture Contexts.*

After my project proposal was accepted, my first step was to share my project ideas with my local congregation. Ninety percent of the membership was excited about the possibilities of this project and what it might mean for the local church. However, a few were skeptical. One lady called me and said, "Pastor, I know you have a passion for this project, but are you sure that this is the right time for our church to take on this project?" When I asked her what she meant, she said,

"Well, the Black church is the only place where Black people can come and be themselves. When we come to church, we do not have to worry about what other people think of us. If we want to shout, dance, laugh out loud, run around the building, or whatever we want to do, it is understood and accepted by other Black people. If we become multicultural, that would come to an end. I think you should do a survey and see if the other members of the church want to do this. I personally don't because I don't think it is the right time for our church."

I responded,

"I do not know if it is the right time or not. All I know is this is the only time I have." I tried to explain to her that God had given me the vision and for that reason, "I must work the works of him that has called me while it is day, for when night comes no one can work."   (John 9:4)

She responded, "Ok, pastor." Opportunity arose for the issue to come up in Bible study as I was teaching about reconciliation. I told the congregation that the issue had been presented to me. I opened the floor for discussion, and one man asked to speak. I gave him the floor. He said to me before the congregation:

"Pastor, I have as a Black man had some very unpleasant experiences with White men. I know how to control myself around them, but I do not trust them. However, no White man will come in my church and tell me how to worship God or how to act or what to do! I'm telling you that right now!"

I asked him to tell me his story, and he was happy to share it with me. While I could sympathize with him, I told him that Christ died not only for the forgiveness of our sins, but for the forgiveness of the sins of all who would believe in Him. I further explained to him that we had a responsibility to forgive as well. He said unto me, "Well, don't say I did not tell you. You have been warned!" At this point, I thought to myself, no wonder it has been said that the Black church may be the last place integrated. I did not do a survey, but I did have a vote using the show of hands of those who were present. All but four people voted yes to the project.

This man, and who knows how many more Black men, are struggling to hold on to a power center they fear is not available to them anywhere else but in the Black church; and if they hold on to that attitude, I am certain that spiritual integration will be almost impossible. After listening to more concerns such as these, I knew I had to pray for healing to take place in this church. Moreover, I knew I had to expose these men and women to a loving community of Christian men and women of various cultures. So, I chose six of the leading men and four of the leading women and sent them on the Walk to Emmaus. These men and women returned from this spiritual retreat with testimonies and joys that encouraged others, even one of the people mentioned above, to want to give my vision a try. I was freed to do what was needed to finish this project. It's amazing how the Emmaus Walk was building a community without even being aware of it.

Once my Church gave their approval, I contacted the pastors of each church that had accepted my request, and the preaching dates were set as follows: the first sermon was preached July 21, 2013 at a local AME Church in Garland, TX; the second sermon was preached July 28, 2013 at a local UMC in Mabank, TX; the third sermon was preached September 29, 2013 at a local UMC in Mesquite, TX; the fourth sermon was preached October 6, 2013 at a local Fellowship church in Dallas, TX; and the fifth sermon was preached November 10, 2013 at a local Hispanic church in Garland, TX.

It was now time to complete the evaluation questionnaire. So, I worked with my advisor on the wording of the questionnaire. When I had a questionnaire that she thought would meet the needs of this project, she gave me her approval to move forward. At this point, the questionnaire consisted of five short-answer questions and five essays questions. I sent the questionnaire to my field supervisor who suggested the form be shortened and more objective. She felt more people would participate in the evaluation if it did not look like it would take a lot of writing to complete it. My field supervisor suggested I change it to include some multiple-choice, true/false and/or scale-type questions. As a result, I divided the evaluation into four questions that could be answered with a yes or no answer; four short answer questions that required a hearing of the message to answer; and three questions that were to be answered using a scale with the following rankings:1–excellent; 2–good; 3–average; 4–poor; 5–unsatisfactory. After redesigning the form, I sent it back to my advisor and field-supervisor informing them of the changes. They both approved the changes.

The next phase involved interviewing three Black female pastors assigned to churches that have a diverse cultural back ground from their original cultural settings.

Interviewing Black Female Pastors Who Pastor in A White Cultural Context

The next phase involved interviewing three Black female pastors assigned to churches that have a diverse cultural back ground from their original cultural settings. The first step of the interview process was to get acquainted with these three women. The next step involved two main questions. The first question addressed what resistance they faced and what they had learned from these resistances. The second question involved sermon preparation and delivery. I wanted to know how they prepared and delivered the preached word in their ministry setting. Because they asked me not to use their names, the participants will be called Pastor A, Pastor B, and Pastor C.

These interviews took place in two settings. The first meeting was around a lunch table in my home. At this meeting, the four of us sat at lunch and got acquainted with each other. The conversation at this gathering was for the purpose of sharing personal information. After we had finished getting acquainted, we began talking about what it is like to be female pastors. The conversation then moved to each of the three pastors sharing with me what it is like to pastor in a diverse cultural context than their own. Before they left my home, I told them I would call them individually to further discuss their

[110]

sermon preparation and the resistance they face in gaining a hearing.

While my first question did address the resistance, they experienced in gaining a hearing of the preached word, my next questions were all dependent on their responses to the first question. Consequently, each person had a diverse set of questions. Since my Book is about preaching and gaining a hearing, I will only share comments about resistances that affect the hearing of the preached word. Though there were many resistances that were the result of prejudices against race, gender and administrative authority, this project was not designed to test those areas of ministry. Therefore, issues of racial profiling, stereotyping, slurring, and prejudices will not be addressed nor, will I address the debate as to whether or not God calls women to preach. The purpose of this Book is to develop sermonic strategies to help Black female preachers overcome resistance to gaining a hearing when preaching in various cultural contexts.

Interview Number 1

Pastor A was the first person I called. She is about sixty-two years old. She has pastored six congregations in her twenty-two years of pastoring. Her first three pastoral charges were in predominantly Black churches and her last three pastoral charges were in predominantly White churches. She is now the senior pastor of a small influential White church in a rural area in Texas. Her average membership is made up of about fifty adults and several youths. She grew up in a Black Baptist church, but in order to pursue her ministry, she changed her denomination to Methodist. She has a M. Div. degree and she has a PhD in Biblical Studies. While she was in seminary, she attended a predominately Caucasian church. She indicated that biblically she learned more in the four years she attended the Caucasian church than she learned in all her life as a member of the Black Baptist church. She believes this may be because of the fact she was in seminary and studying theology, but for whatever the reason she knew this church appealed more to her intellect than the Black church she had attended for the majority of her Christian life.

When I asked her if she thought Caucasian churches were better than Black churches, she responded, "No, I do not." She continued by saying, "I just believe one should experience spiritual growth both emotionally and mentally. The Black church fed my emotions, but at that time in my life I needed more. Now I know why." I knew she was referring to her pastoral charge. In her opinion, there is more biblical teaching in the Caucasian church than in the Black church. She further states, it has been her experience that in Caucasian churches there is a greater focus on doctrine, evangelism, discipleship and mission than one would find in the Black church. So, her preaching has a different focus than most Black female preachers.

When asked about her resistances, she indicated that her resistance mainly centers on cultural difference in worship. Having been brought up in the Black church, she was accustomed to sometimes waving her hands or standing up when the choir sang songs that appealed to her emotions. She is also an accomplished musician who sometimes likes to play and sing the sermonic selection or the invitational hymn. These worship traits were met with much resistance. The church she now pastors told her that was not acceptable. This resistance interferes with her spiritual or mental preparation for preaching. Her motive for physically participating in worship is to usher in the Holy Spirit or to feel the presence of the Holy Spirit before she speaks the Word of God. Being denied this privilege is a hindrance to her worship experience, which plays a major role in her preaching.

When asked what she does to overcome this resistance, she confessed that she had learned to pick her battles. It has taken her some time to do so, but she has learned how to hold her peace and focus on other things. Her strategies for overcoming resistance are to quietly accept the ways of her congregation while leading them into worship, and then to find herself a Black church in the afternoon where she could praise

God in the spirit and truth of her culture. In other words, changing her ways did not change her, it just made her more effective in what she was called to do.

Like Paul, so that she might reach them with the Word of God, she learned how to adjust her style of preaching and worshiping to complement the ways and thoughts of her hearers while she was in their cultural context.

> Though I am free and belong to no one, I have made myself a slave to everyone, to win as many as possible. 20 To the Jews I became like a Jew, to win the Jews. To those under the law I became like one under the law (though I myself am not under the law), so as to win those under the law. 21 To those not having the law I became like one not having the law (though I am not free from God's law but am under Christ's law), so as to win those not having the law. 22 To the weak I became weak, to win the weak. I have become all things to all people so that by all possible means I might save some. 23 I do all this for the sake of the gospel that I may share in its blessings. 1 Corinthians 9:19-23

This is not to say she acted one way with one group of people and a different way with another group. This is not what Paul did nor is it what I gathered she did. I believe Paul wrote

[114]

this to say that sometimes to reach others with the truth of the Gospel, you must use their beliefs and their ways as a method of understanding. For example, in order to reach the religious Jews, who believed in the law, he used the law and spoke the truth to them on their terms. However, when he was speaking to the gentiles, he would not use the law but rather he would rely on his integrity and culture to relate the good news to them. This is a good strategy.

When I asked her about sermon preparation, she commented that her main focus in that area is to make sure she correctly teaches the Word of God. She seems comfortable with her method of preaching because she is a lecturer and most of her congregation prefers teaching over preaching. The resistance here is limited because those who did not want to be taught by a Black female have moved their membership elsewhere. She says, "Praise God! That is a battle I do not have to fight." Because of her education and her understanding of what it is like to preach to a Bible-teaching and Bible-believing church, she does not have any resistance in gaining a hearing from those who come to hear a word of truth. However, she believes the same message preached the same way in a Black congregation, whose focus is mainly on anointing, deliverance and prosperity, would not be accepted in the same manner. Thus, the resistance she avoids in this situation is the habit of most Black preachers, to replace doctrine with emotionalism.

When preparing sermons, Pastor A mainly relies on a thorough interaction and exegesis of the scriptures. Because she is not preaching with the expectation of getting people to shout, she has no need to leave room for celebration in her message. Her expectation from the preached word involves reaching people with a word from God, based on the doctrines of God that will drive them forward into evangelism, discipleship, and mission. While I know these are important aspects of ministry, my focus in this project is on gaining a hearing when preaching Christ-centered message. So, I concluded the conversation at this point and thanked her for her time.

From our conversation, I would assume that Pastor A is a doctrinal preacher. Based on the needs of her congregation, she preaches doctrine with intent to transform, touch and relate how the Word of God can bring about a change in the mindset of the congregation, for the purpose of making them better citizens of the Kingdom of God. The Bible says, "be not conformed by this world, but be ye transformed by the renewing of your mind" (Romans 12:2). I believe Pastor A's strategy to overcome the resistance she faces in preaching in a culture different from her own is to put forth an extra effort to show how the doctrines of the church can promote the coming of the Kingdom of God in the daily lives of the members of her congregation.

As a Black female preacher, this is a gift that I do not have. While I believe it is important we know the doctrines of the church, I find it is difficult for me to preach the doctrines. While I do not believe the doctrines of the church should be ignored, I believe preaching should bring about a change in the moral and ethical beliefs of both the saved and unsaved hearers. I also believe that Christians should be intellectually knowledgeable about what they should believe but preaching doctrine to the lost may confuse them even more. However, if the preacher can show experientially how these doctrines make a difference in the lives of the hearers and why the doctrine matters in their ecclesial tradition, I think they should by all means go ahead and preach the doctrine. Conversely, because I feel preaching doctrine is not a strategy that is cross-cultural, I still believe it is easier to teach the doctrine, giving the audience opportunity to ask questions, than to preach it.

Interview Number 2

The second person I interviewed was Pastor B. She is a Black female who serves as an assistant pastor in a suburban city located south of Dallas. She has a Master of Divinity degree and serves in the ministry position of pastoral care. She had worshipped as a lay member of a Black church until she graduated from seminary and was assigned to this Caucasian church. She has been the associate pastor at this church for ten years. Her ministry is pastoral care, but she teaches confirmation classes and preaches on occasion.

A few years ago, because of the illness of the senior pastor, Pastor B was placed in a position in which she had to preach every Sunday for about 18 months. When asked about gaining a hearing from her listeners, she also stated that she believes in preparation, intense study of the scriptures, and a solid exegesis of the text. However, in her opinion there is much more to preaching then just the study and preparation phase. She states: "I know some women who think the preaching is the easiest part of ministry. However, I feel there is a whole lot more to preaching then just getting in the pulpit and talking for 20 minutes." She believes that preaching must include sound theology, a biblical witness and a contemporary experience. In other words, because she spends most of her time in pastoral care, she believes the preached word should reach the heart of the listeners as well as the mind.

When I asked her how she does that in the cultural context in which she preaches, she said "Ella. I am a Black female. I have not forgotten the struggle, nor have I forgotten what it is like to suffer, to have pain and sorrows. While I am theologically trained and intellectually prepared, I understand there is more to preaching then just me." She implied that she never depends solely on her preparation. When she enters the pulpit, she gives what she has prepared over to God and depends on the Holy Spirit to guide her into what to say and what not to say in that preaching moment.

When I asked if she stood behind the pulpit to preach, her response was sometimes but not always. She begins behind the podium, but as the Spirit moves her, her mannerisms change. She asserted that because the people know her in a personable way, they relate to her while she is preaching. Therefore, she looks at the audience and as the Spirit interacts with her, she interacts with the people.

When asked if she whooped, she said: "No, I have never enjoyed the whoop myself. I usual tune the preacher out when they start that. I do not find that necessary. It is to get an emotional response in some churches, but I don't see the purpose. However, I do use gestures, inflections, illustrations and emphases at different points in the sermon." She further suggested that the intensity of the whoop is often placed at the end of a sermon but is better placed throughout the sermon at different intervals. When I asked her what strategy, she uses in her sermon preparation and the preaching moment, she concluded that sermon preparation and the preaching moment should consist of a communion with the Holy Spirit that comes through the studying of the Bible and constant prayer life combined with personal application.

When I asked her about how important the cross and resurrection of Jesus was in her preaching, she said: "Ella, the cross is not just a Black thing. The Black church uses the cross as an instrument of encouragement for the poor, unemployed, and uneducated, but the cross of Jesus is meant to encourage the lost and perishing that there is a God who loves and cares for them, too. The cross and resurrection also reminds those of us who are already believers in Christ that we need to become more mature in our understanding of why Jesus died on a cross and rose from the grave, so that those who believe may receive the forgiveness and reconciliation necessary for salvation. That is what I needed to hear. I thanked her, and we ended the conversation.

Interview Number 3

My final interview was with a young Black woman, freshly out of Bright Theological Seminary. She is 27 years old and is excited and on fire about being able to have her own pastoral charge. Presently, she is serving in her first year as an assistant pastor at a Christian Church in the DFW area. She has only preached three times, but says she had a wonderful experience on each occasion. The membership at her small church has about 200 members.

Our conversation was really short because she has very limited experience. Her main comments had to do with integration. Being young, she had not experienced any of the racial slurs and racial difficulties that some of the other interviewees had encountered. She has attended Black churches before, but she chose the Caucasian church because she says that a high view of scripture and sound doctrine and expository Bible teaching is more important to her than comfortable worship styles. In her opinion, "God has placed me in this predominantly Caucasian church because my presence here adds to the diversification of the church." She explains that while the church is different from her culture, it is a blessing to worship in a place where she can grow. She said, she has had many unique experiences while fellowshipping with this church. She believes her "burning desire for the truth of the word of God and the zeal to share the word of God is a great match for the place in which she has made her choice to serve the Lord." In other words, her presence at this church is helping other ethnicities learn how to interact with Blacks.

When asked about the sermons she's preached, the thing that was the most challenging for her was to be able to contextualize the Gospel for those other Blacks within the community. Her opinion of most Black preaching is that it is old-school stuff that came from the time of slavery. WOW! That statement made me think about my style of preaching. For this style of preaching that I have did come from traditional Black church preaching. It is what I grew up with. It is what we kids used to do on Sunday evenings when we imitated the old Black preacher from the church. I only attended church about three times a year, but I could imitate the preacher as well as anyone else. We were having fun back then, but now I still preach the same way, only with more knowledge about what I am saying.

In her opinion, the cultural reason for Black preaching style is the ties it has to the songs that the slaves used to sing in the field. I asked her what she knew about slavery and what the church was doing at that time. She said she had watched a documentary on the History Channel a few years ago, and she remembered it very vividly.

When I asked her what she felt while she was in worship, she said that emotions are a part of her worship setting. She continued by saying that along with emotions, you must have character and passion. I did not catch it at the time, but since I have talked about it in this book, I know now she was talking about Aristotle's rhetorical persuasions. Without those three things, she says you cannot tell others what Christ has done for us. "For us?" I was not about to open that can of worms with this young lady. But I sure wanted to know what she meant when she said, "What Christ has done for us."

Instead, I went to my next question. I asked her about her sermon preparation and delivery. She said, "I prefer expository preaching over motivational speeches and sing/talk sermons that I hear in Black churches on YouTube and television." Expository preaching, she said, "is the fundamental method of properly exegeting the Word of God. It is what is needed to help the preacher keep focused on what God has done through Jesus Christ and to keep her focus off of self-centered man." She says she stands on Paul's advice, in which he has instructed young preachers "to study to show themselves approved.... rightly dividing the word of truth." She says, "in order to become spiritual, one has to become more scriptural." "Too many Black preachers," she says, "put their emphasis on being spiritual, spirit-filled and anointed, instead of being scriptural."

I was so ready for this conversation to be over. However, I had to ask myself why this young lady was irritating me so much. I love the Black church. I was really offended by her implying that the Black church is really just a shouting, non-scripturally founded and uneducated church. Nevertheless, my purpose of interviewing her was not to correct, persuade or instruct, but it was to learn from her. So, I listened attentively to everything she had to say.

My opinion of this interviewee is that she believes most Black churches have replaced sound doctrine with emotionalism. She's not saying everyone has to do expository preaching, but she does believe whatever form of preaching is done, it must be sound in doctrine. She believes expository preaching helps the preacher to stay away from poor theological doctrines. I will say more about my opinion of this interviewee in my critical evaluation.

Steps in Sermon Preparation

Because I am a manuscript preacher, my next step was to begin writing the sermon. The second church at which I would be preaching was doing a series on the miracles of Jesus. I was given a list of the miracles the pastor was preaching from and was asked to select a different passage to preach from. I chose to preach from the miracle of Jesus healing a woman in the synagogue, as presented in Luke's Gospel, Luke 13:10-17. I studied this passage of scripture and prayed for guidance from the Holy Spirit for four weeks before I started preparing the sermon. During those four weeks, I decided on the theme for the message: "Praising God for His Goodness to Mankind." I focused on this theme at each preaching engagement.

Much is involved in understanding the cultural context of a church. So, there are many developments contributing to the sermonic strategies required for a Black female preacher to gain a hearing in various cultural contexts. Despite that fact, this Book seeks to prove that preaching Christ-centered messages in various cultural contexts is still possible, if the preacher invests the time necessary for understanding both the biblical text as well as the cultural context. To proclaim the Gospel in any given cultural context, one must be able to biblically exegete the text. However, a biblical exegesis alone is not enough. I feel that once one has become familiar with the text, the preacher then needs to mentally experience the text based on the culture in which it will be preached. According to Kevin Vanhoozer in his book, *Everyday Theology: How to Read Cultural Texts and Interpret Trends*, Christians should be able to exegete both the Bible and the culture. He states on page sixteen:

> The reason why theology must study God *and* contemporary culture is the same reason why preaching must connect both with the biblical text and the listener's context: because disciples do not follow the gospel in a vacuum but wend their Christian way through particular times and places, each with its own problem and possibilities.[40]

I agree that the preacher must be familiar with both the text and the culture. Thus, since my Book seeks to identify sermonic strategies that will help a Black female preacher gain

---

[40]Kevin J. Vanhoozer, Charles A. Anderson, Michael J. Sleasman, *Everyday Theology: How to Read Cultural Texts and Interpret Trends*, (Baker Academic, a division of Baker Publishing Group.) 2007. P16

a hearing as an agent of God when preaching in various cultural contexts, my next step in this sermon preparation was to do a Biblical and cultural exegesis.

Exegesis of the Biblical Text using Dialogical Teaching

As a means of becoming familiar with the text, during this four-week period I also taught from this passage of scripture in my Bible study classes. The purpose for this strategy was to enter into dialogical session with the congregation to get feedback about how this passage of scripture related to them and their experiences or encounters with God. William Brosend in his book, *The Preaching of Jesus: Gospel Proclamation, Then and Now*, writes about the use of dialogical preaching. A short definition of dialogical preaching is this: Dialogical preaching responds to the challenges and questions of both the preacher and his or her listeners as they engage the sermon's text. Brosend further explains that in dialogical preaching, Jesus not only responded to specific spoken questions, He also responded by drawing on scripture, tradition and culture. In my opinion, scripture is very important in preaching. However, in sermon preparation, one is not just to read and interpret the scriptures. The primary purpose of reading the scriptures is to interpret life through the reading of the scriptures. Brosend writes, "Dialogical preaching is not about our speaking, but about their hearing."[41]

As I understand it, such dialogue often occurs in a small group setting. I used this praxis in my Wednesday night Bible study classes, and I taught from the Luke13:10-17 text of scripture for four weeks. However, because the average attendance on Wednesday nights is less than ten percent of our Sunday attendees, we did not have a good representation of the whole congregation. Yet, among those in attendance, I found we had a great dialogical discussion, in most cases about the meaning, purpose and application of the text. It was interesting to notice, as we shared ideas and wrestled with some of the same issues and questions, how almost all of us would leave the study feeling a sense of accomplishment and understanding.

For those who participated in these Bible study discussions, many have confessed that having the opportunity to dialogue about the meaning, history and purpose of these issues enabled them to have a better understanding of the sermon when they heard it. But the question that lingered in my mind was whether or not the other ninety percent of the congregation, who were not in attendance on Wednesday nights, would be getting the same understanding from the sermon. So, I expanded this theory into other small group settings, such as: the men and women's groups, youth groups

---

[41]William Brosend, *The Preaching of Jesus: Gospel Proclamation, Then and Now*, (Westminster John Knox Press; 1 edition February 2010) p.30.

and lay meetings. Because most of these groups are led by laity and have a teaching format that includes a period of personal questions and answers, the best way for me to benefit from this strategy was to have the group leaders teach from the same preaching text and then share with me the concerns, needs, and questions of the members of the group. From their responses to these questions, I was able to conclude that dialoguing not only helps the congregation's understanding of the preached word, it also helps the preacher prepare sermons that are relevant to the hearers.

Again, for the purpose of this project, I taught this passage of scripture, Luke 13:10-17, for four weeks straight. The first week we focused on the role of the woman in the text. The second week's focus was on the presence of Jesus in the text. The third week's focus was on the religious leaders, and the fourth week's focus was on the crowd in the text. In these four studies, the people shared what the text said to them about each situation and how this information applied to their lives. This exegesis did not use Bible commentaries or dictionaries. It was done strictly from Bible study classes, personal examples and experiences of the congregation. It was also done with the cultural exegesis in mind.

I shared in story form my Biblical knowledge and wisdom that has been gained from years of studying the scriptures and recently from this text, then I asked the students for feedback. During these Bible study classes, we looked at this text, word by word, line by line, and verse by verse. Each Bible study class lasted at least two hours. The age of the participants ranged from 14 to 92. Each student was given an opportunity to share his/her opinion of the text. Each student was asked to take notes in any form they wished. So that everyone would be encouraged to participate, there was no structure to this note-taking process. There were no names attached to the notes. This was simply a brain-storming session that took place during these Bible study meetings. After I collected the notes, my advisory team and I separated them into sections. The first section was notes taken on the woman, the second section were notes taken on Jesus, the third section were notes taken on the religious leaders, and the last section were notes taken on the multitude of people that were there in the synagogue that day.

Thus, the exegesis will be a list of bullet points of common notes that were taken from each of the above-referenced characters in the story. From this list of bullet points, I and the advisory team looked at each church's cultural exegesis and decided which of these points would be best to express in each church. This was done through a process of elimination. I have included an abbreviated version of this exegesis in this book. The whole exegesis would take too much space; therefore, I have chosen what I thought was important to include. After the cultural and Biblical exegesis was finalized, I wrote each sermon. I preached the sermon, collected the sermon evaluations and made a statistical report of the findings. There were five sermons preached, but only three of these sermons were evaluated with the written survey. The other two sermons were sermons I preached by invitation and will not be included in the statistics.

Cultural Context Exegesis

Another area of resistance I had to avoid was that of speaking of victories and defeats without knowing the moral, social, economic and ethnic conditions of the particular church's cultural context. For example, if there were a lot of issues dealing with divorces, parental difficulties, unemployment, etc., in the church, talking about the victories in this area might not be a wise decision. In fact, it could be insulting, thereby causing the hearers to close their ears and minds to anything I might have to say afterwards. While this type of message may be powerfully effective in my cultural setting, the effect might have a different impact on hearers in other cultures. Therefore, before I could really plan the sermons for each church I was to preach in, I had to know something about the culture and the way of life for each individual church.

In my first Doctor of Ministry class, I learned the term "cultural exegesis." This term was mostly used in reference to missional churches. However, because I believe a sermon should reflect our cultural understanding, I find that a cultural exegesis can also be helpful in sermon preparation, especially when one is preaching outside his/her cultural context. A cultural exegesis can be helpful in bridging the gap between the preacher and the audience he/she is trying to reach with the Gospel message. In other words, a cultural exegesis helps one to study the culture of the church so one can answer questions pertaining to the who, what, when and where of that culture. Knowing the answers to these questions allows one to contextualize the Gospel message so the hearers can better understand its relationship to their everyday lives. Aubrey Malphurs, in his book, *Planting Growing Churches for the 21st Century,* writes about the importance of cultural exegesis for maintaining cultural relevance in the church:

> A vital aspect of communicating divine truth is the application of truth to life. This can't take place, however, unless we understand what's taking place in people's lives, both lost and saved … To study what's taking place in the "world out there" and to address it in terms of God's truth will help add

[42]Aubrey Malphurs, *Planting Growing Churches for the 21st Century,* (Baker Books, MI, 1998), 174.

authenticity to sermons—whether they're directed to lost or saved people.[42]

Therefore, to gain insight into the cultural context of each church, I had a brief conversation with each pastor of each church before I prepared the sermon.

There were only two churches I preached in that I did not know anything about, so the cultural exegesis was only done for those two congregations. Since I was not planning to become the pastor of these churches, this cultural exegesis was limited. Further, since my purpose for the cultural exegesis focused on making the sermon relative to the cultural context of that church, I only addressed questions that were relevant to the people's language, interests and customs in that church. In other words, I mainly wanted to know what they were interested in, what made them excited and what attracted them to the church. Therefore, through conversations with the pastors of these churches, I paid close attention to what they said about their respective congregations' hopes, dreams, struggles, and challenges.

The way to do a cultural exegesis is to observe and view the cultural influences of a particular culture from their perspective, rather than from one's own cultural views. In Tom Steffens's book, *Reconnecting God's Story to Ministry: Cross Cultural Storytelling at Home and Abroad*, gives the following list of questions one can use to help in exegeting the cultural context:

> What is the worldview of the target audience?
>
> What is the culture's decision-making pattern?
>
> What does it cost a person in this culture to become a Christian?
>
> What redemptive analogy is best for this culture?
>
> How does this culture view Christianity?
>
> What does the culture know about the basic components of the gospel story?
>
> Is this culture based on shame or guilt?
>
> How will this culture understand Christian rituals?
>
> What is the best delivery system for exposing people of this culture to the gospel?[43]

These kinds of questions are said to be of help to preachers who are seeking to preach the truth of the Gospel in a culturally understandable manner.

Many more resistances exist of which one must be aware when preaching in diverse cultural contexts, but I think the above questions are the most important to keep in mind when doing sermon preparation. To prepare for these preaching

---

[43]Thomas A. Steffen and David J. Hasslegrave, *Reconnecting God's Story to ministry: Cross Cultural storytelling at Home and Abroad*, La Habra: Center for Organization and Ministry, 1997; quoted in Stetzer, *Planting Missional Churches*, (Broadman and Holman Publishing, Nashville, TN. 2006), 34.

assignments, I took time to assess the churches' cultural positions, to pray for the leading of the Holy Spirit, and to learn from previous mistakes. Keeping these resistances ever before me, I tried to find points of this text that would be familiar and acceptable in any cultural context. After identifying my resistances, I was now ready to begin my exegesis of the text.

Sermon Exegesis in the Form of a Story

In this story of the woman who is bent over, I see two things. There is a confrontation between Jesus and the religious leaders about the laws of the Sabbath. There is also a story in this text about liberation. The context of this story takes place around the teachings of Jesus. In this specific incident, Jesus is on his way to Jerusalem. Because it was Sunday, he stopped in Samaria and went into the synagogue to teach. Two things happened while Jesus was in Samaria in this synagogue. In the first part of the story, Jesus saw a woman with a condition, and he healed her. The scene looks like this, Jesus goes into the synagogue to teach, he sees someone who needs help, he calls this person to him, he touches her, and she is healed. After she is healed, she stands up and glorifies God, or in some versions, she praises God.

The second part of this story revolves around a controversy which takes place among those in the synagogue who became indignant because Jesus healed the woman on the

Sabbath. Part three of this story revolves around the religious leaders' response to the healing. They were also upset that Jesus healed the woman on the Sabbath. However, instead of addressing Jesus about the miracle, they confronted the people who were witnessing the miracle. This leads to the fourth part of this story, which is Jesus's response to the religious leaders. This confrontation causes Jesus to respond not only to those who became indignant but to all who were in the synagogue. He confronted them about God's love for people and about the purpose of the Sabbath. The final part of this story revolves around the crowd's response to Jesus's shaming the religious leaders. The Bible says they praised Jesus for the wonderful things he was doing.

Historically, this text is set in the context of Judaism. During this time, the Jewish leaders had very strict rules about disrespecting the Sabbath. In fact, the Sabbath was the foundation of the Jewish identity. The Pharisees were especially protective of the Sabbath law. Jesus was constantly trying to teach the Pharisees that God cared more about the people than he did about things. He was also trying to teach them that the time to help somebody is when they need the help, not when the law says it is permissible to help. Jesus was also trying to teach these Pharisees that it was better to worship God than be instruments of God.

So, in closing, what we have in this story is a combination of a miraculous healing and a controversy. The movement of the story is as follows: teaching or worship, a miracle, a celebration of the miracle, a controversy over the miracle, a conflict from the miracle, a resolution of the conflict, and finally a rejoicing of the church. Following my outlining of the story, the congregation was asked to participate in identifying the roles of the characters in the text. Please see in the Appendices section the outline in bullet point form of the results of brainstorming that took place in the four Bible Study classes. My task after the exegesis was to decide which episode of this story I wanted to focus on. I had six choices: praise, teaching, miracle, conflict, consequence of the conflict and celebration. I decided my theme would be praise. The woman praised God after she was healed, and the crowd praised Jesus for His wonderful works.

Preaching Engagements

I did an extensive Biblical exegesis of this text, and I kept every note I wrote, with the understanding that I could not preach it all in any one sermon. However, since I had a good database of information on this text, I was able to adapt the text and relate it to the cultural setting in which I would be preaching. Before each preaching engagement I would take the prepared sermon and adapt its content according to the information I received from each pastor, the cultural exegesis, the Biblical exegesis, the list of resistances, and the leading of the Holy Spirit. After this preparation, I would trust God for a message that was fit for the culture in which I would be preaching.

After the sermon was outlined and the dates for preaching were set, I sent the evaluation and an introductory letter to each of the participating pastors and evaluators, asking them to distribute it to at least twelve volunteers in advance of hearing the sermon. After I had preached, the completed evaluations were then sent to me by email or postal mail within the following week. I filed them in categories of gender, culture and age. After each sermon, I reviewed the information, collected the statistics from the data, and drew a conclusion of the matter. The sermon outline, evaluation form, selected answers to evaluation from each church, and exegesis may be found in the Appendices section.

Church Number One –AME Church; Garland, TX

The first church in which I preached this sermon was a AME Church in Garland on July 21, 2013. The church in which I have been assigned as the pastor. Every year we have what we call "Friend and Family Day." I invited my friends from diverse cultures to attend this friend and family day celebration. While the purpose for this celebration is primarily a fundraiser, it is fun fellowshipping with our family and

[137]

friends as we worship together and then eat together in a big celebration. Many of the people whom I invited are people I have met while doing my Emmaus Walks, retreats, and women's conferences. They have heard me preach or speak within their contexts and want to hear me preach in my own context. So, this is always a big event.

The church holds about two hundred fifty people comfortably. There were no less than three hundred fifty and possibly as many as four hundred people crammed into that building on this date. Our tiny little HVAC unit was not built for this mass of people, and so it was hot beyond measure in that room. But no one left. There were people from the front door all the way up to the communion table, with all four of the isles having a row of seats in them. The choir stand, and pulpit were filled. We had been in worship for two hours before I stood to preach. But, finally the preaching moment arrived. The topic for that Sunday was "Praising God for the Wonderful Things He Has Done." For this sermon, the main points were:

1. The one who received the blessing.
2. The one who gave the blessing.
3. The ones who witnessed the blessings.

The focus of this message was the assumption that we were gathered together in church, and among us there were many people standing in the need of a blessing. We need to realize that Jesus is in our midst, and He is ready to heal us, forgive us, restore us, and reunite us together as family and friends. However, as wonderful as this might be, there are people around you who will not be happy that Jesus has restored you in one way or another. But, in spite of that, if Jesus blesses you today, go ahead and give him the praise. Don't wait until you leave, you can praise him right now. At that call and response, there were people who stood to praise God, people who waved their hands, people who had tears rolling down their faces, people who shouted and screamed with release and with joy, people who sat with their mouths open in amazement, and people who were wondering what was happening in that place. What was demonstrated on this Sunday was a typical African American worship context and setting. Everyone enjoyed themselves despite the differences that we may have had.

There were twenty-nine evaluations turned in from this occasion. The following are the statistics of those evaluations. Of the twenty-nine evaluations turned in, there were six men (21%) and twenty-three women (79%). Ethnically, nine were Black (31%), fifteen were White (52%) and five were Hispanic (17%). The ages represented were: four in the age group of 20-40 (14%), eighteen in the age group 41-60 (62%), six in the age group 61-80 (21%) and one in the age group over 80 (3%).

The following written response represents the average response from each church. Question Number One - The Biblical Text had two questions: Was the sermon's theological claim faithful to selected text? Did the text really make a difference for this sermon? All respondents from all three churches answered yes to both questions (100%).

Church Number Two – A UMC; Mabank, TX

The second church in which I preached this sermon was a United Methodist Church in Mabank, TX. There were over two-hundred fifty people in attendance that day. I had intended for this to be the predominately White congregation. However, there was a diversity of people in the congregation on that particular Sunday. So again, I preached to a multi-cultural congregation at this church. I have been preaching at this UMC in Mabank every year now for the last 10 years. The people at this UMC Mabank and I have a very special relationship. I have traveled with them on mission trips to Mexico; they were very helpful in helping me build the sanctuary for Agape Temple AME church; when I was struggling financially they were very instrumental in helping me to make ends meet; and my first year of seminary was paid for by this church. So, I know quite a bit culturally about this UMC in Mabank as well as spiritually. The church was doing a series on the miracles of Jesus. For this visit, they asked that I do the same. Because I was doing a sermon on the miracles of Jesus for this church, I chose the same text for the other churches.

Because of the relationship we have and their knowledge of my personal struggle, I chose as the sermon topic "The Story behind My Praise." The points of the sermon were:

1. As a daughter of Abraham, the bent woman was an heir to a promise.
2. She was broken down on her way to her promise.
3. Jesus touched her; she was healed and praised God.

The message focused on the fact that many times on our way to our promise we suffer something or go through something; but, because Jesus is faithful, we are delivered from those things. Sometimes, it may appear that our deliverance is not coming; but with patience, perseverance and praise, we eventually reach our destination. In other words, if we remain faithful, Jesus will eventually see our devotion, call us forward and touch us. Along the way to the destination, God will send us help. There are always some people that love God who will help the children of God in times of difficulty. These same people will rejoice with you when you have been set free from your bondage. However, there are always those who do not want to see you victorious because they themselves are still in bondage. But, you do not have to fight these people, you can leave them to Jesus. Jesus knows how to handle those who will become indignant because of your deliverance or healing. All you must do is remember what God has done through Jesus Christ and give God the praise.

As I gave personal testimony, the people were in one accord with me because they had been with me during the time of the struggles that related to the examples I gave. I ended this sermon by singing two versus of the song, *Shackled by a Heavy Burden*, better known as, *He Touched Me*. The people rejoiced with me in this conclusion.

There were thirty-six people who responded to the survey from this church, which consisted of ten men (28%) and twenty-six women (72%). The following are the statistics of those evaluations. Ethnically, four were Black (11%), twenty-two were White (61%), two were Hispanic (6%) and eight were Asians (22%). The ages represented were: sixteen in the age group of 20-40 (44%), twelve in the age group 41-60 (33%), eight in the age group 61-80 (22%) and zero in the age group over 80 (0%).

Church Number Three – A UMC; Mesquite, TX

The preaching engagement at this UMC; in Mesquite, Texas was an invitation to preach a church anniversary. It was not originally a part of the planned preaching engagements. However, since this UMC engagement in Mabank turned out to be a diverse worship setting, I included this UMC, in Mesquite in the project as a predominately Caucasian church. With the exception of one man who was of African descendant, all other attendees were Caucasian. There was no cultural exegesis done on this church.

The evaluations were presented on the Sunday of the message. There were only eight people who chose to participate in the survey. Of those eight participants only three put their age on the survey. 100% of the participants were Caucasian. However, because only three of them gave their gender, I do not know the percentage of male and female participants. Of the eight people who took the survey, 100% answered yes to all the objective questions. Three of the participants gave written responses to the questions, as included in the Appendices of this document. Some of the people visited with me during the luncheon after the ceremony and shared how they enjoyed the message. I do not think evaluations from this church would contribute much to this project analysis. Regardless, I have included them in the Appendices.

Because this was their church anniversary, my focus on this sermon was on the benefits of attending church. The major points of this sermon were:

1. Jesus went to church on the Sabbath

2. A woman who had been sick for 18 years was devoted to worship on Sunday

3. Jesus and the woman met at church and lives were changed.

Church Number Four – A Local Fellowship Church; Dallas, TX

The fourth preaching engagement was also not a planned engagement. I am a part of this local fellowship church that meets on the first Sunday afternoon of each month. The scheduled preacher was not able to preach on this Sunday afternoon, and I was asked to preach in her place. Since I had already preached this message three times, I could preach it from memory. So, without notes, preparation or exegesis, I stood and preached this message from my heart. This was an all-Black congregation; therefore, I could just relax and be myself. I preached this message, and the church caught on fire with the Holy Spirit. People were shouting, people were jumping, and people were dancing in the Spirit. I had fun preaching this message. It was like the message came alive in my life, as well as in the lives of these hearers. For my sermon topic on this Sunday, I used the words of the familiar song, *"Praise Is What I Do!"*

The points of this message were:

1. I'll lift my hands in praise whenever I am close to you.

2. I'll praise you whether I am happy or sad.

3. I'll praise you while I can.

There were no evaluation forms, and there are no statistical reports to be made; but in this case, I believe the response of the people evaluated and validated the sermon in its own way. I am getting happy right now, just thinking about the excitement of that day. The Holy Spirit came in that place that day and had His way in the lives of the people who were in attendance. Of all the previous times in which this message was preached, no one responded to the message by invitation. But, on this day there were three people who gave their lives to Christ. There were many that came to the altar for prayer. The Holy Ghost was alive and well and active in changing the lives of the congregation on that particular date. I asked myself what made the difference? I believe I let go and let God have the message on that Sunday. My focus and my intentions were strictly pointing toward Jesus and how worthy He is to be praised. When I thought about all Jesus had done for me, I allowed the Holy Spirit to use my words of appreciation on that day to bless the house. Hallelujah! What a time we had in the Lord.

Church Number Five – A Hispanic Church; Garland, TX

The last church I preached the message in was a Hispanic church that was using the sanctuary at a local church for worship. This Hispanic church was a starter church and had only twelve people in attendance, including the pastor, his wife and three children. The pastor did his best to interpret the message in Spanish as I spoke it in English. I did not feel that the purpose of this preaching assignment was accomplished. I never felt so alone. It was as if I was in a strange land and viewed as an intruder. The people were friendly, but they were not accepting. My opinion of this worship is that they really did not want me there nor did they want me to preach to them, for whatever reasons, legitimate or not. However, since they were using the facility for free, I think they felt obligated. No evaluation forms were returned from this Hispanic Church. So, there is no report from that church.

Because most of the people who participated in this project are people I know and love, I thought it would be a good idea to invite someone else to preach to this diverse group, so I created and designed a "Unity in Diversity" worship service. Now, as I said I love these people, so I did not want to subject them to any junk food. Therefore, I reached way out there and invited the best Black female preacher I know to deliver the preached word for this occasion. I have mentioned her several times in this book because I tremendously admire Bishop Vashti Murphy McKenzie. She is a phenomenal called-out woman of God. She has achieved so many wonderful accomplishments during her life as an agent of God's communication. But I had not read or heard of any diversity in her ministry. I did not know if she had spoken in any ecumenical setting before this one or not. I really wanted to think surely, she had, but I did not know. Much to my amazement, she said yes and accepted my invitation. I visited with her in her office and shared my vision. Not wanting to tell her what to preach (I mean she is my Bishop after all!), I closed my conversation by saying, "But you don't have to preach that, just preach what you are led to preach." She probably thought I had lost my mind. This woman is a master handler of the Word.

After my visit with her, I began the planning stage of this program. Unlike the other engagements, this was an assignment I had to do myself. The plan was to have a diverse congregation, a diverse worship setting, a diversity of leadership and a diversity of clergy participation in ethnicity as well as in gender. I wanted to do something big. I casually brought the subject up in a steward board meeting at my church. I told them we needed to invite the Bishop to come preach at our church because it would not look good for us if we are the only church that has not at least invited her to our church. There was a total and complete silence, so I jokingly said it was just a spur of the moment thought. They laughed at that comment, but I knew this was something I had to do. If for no other reason, I had to do it because I had already invited her, and she had said yes.

I continued to pray about this service until the Holy Spirit revealed the answer to me. The answer was dollars. At another steward board meeting, I mentioned how wonderful it would be to have another Friend and Family Day type of celebration for our Church Anniversary and how I thought we should invite Bishop McKenzie to come and preach it. Well, Friend and Family Day is our biggest fundraiser event, so immediately they saw dollar signs and said, "Let's do it." I thought, "Thank you, Jesus!" The next thing I did was to contact my friends, Rev. David Weber, Rev. Cathy Partridge, Rev. Joe Pool, Kirk Ragsdale, Nancy Summers, and Jackye Waiters-Lee. The moment they heard the vision they were ready to help. They all thought it was a much-needed Godly vision. I later met with Rev. Cathy Partridge, and we worked out some details. The service was held at First UMC Rockwall to accommodate the anticipated crowd.

It took me three months to plan this event. According to the evaluations, which were freestyle evaluations, the event was a tremendous success. The following letter is given as an example of the kinds of feedback I received. More detailed letters are listed in the Appendices.

Dear Ella,

I attended the worship service on Sunday. Here is what I observed and experienced: The service was very well organized, with the numerous pastors, the music, dance, puppetry, and sermon. Everything was done so well! The energy level in the audience was electric! All the music and the dance had the audience on their feet. The Bishop's sermon presentation was so Dynamic. She was on fire! I personally was hanging on to every word. She preached from her heart and Soul! Lots of emotion and the topic was right on- very timely. I especially liked that we all came together as one body to worship. Lots of love was in the church!! The people I was sitting with had the same reaction as me! Really enjoyed it all! I had never been to an AME service before, it was a wonderful experience!

To sum it up for me - it rocked!!!

Hugs and blessings to you!
Helen Davids

Chapter 5

Critical Evaluation

Introduction

"There is neither Jew nor Greek, there is neither slave nor free, there is neither male nor female, for you are all one in Christ Jesus." (Galatians 3:28) Not very many people like living in tension. Most people will avoid resistance as much as possible. When it comes to where we live, whom we associate with, and even where we worship most of us, if given a choice, will choose comfort over resistance. The main way we pursue this comfort in our relationships is to avoid people who are different from us. So, we live in communities where we know the people are just like us, we socialize in communities where we know we won't be judged, and we worship in communities where we know folk act like us. Bottom line, we all want to be accepted for who we are. Honestly, I see nothing wrong with that. Yet, the truth remains that resistance is something that no one likes, so we try to avoid it at all costs.

As I traveled my way through this Book, I often wondered if Paul were writing today, would he say that there is neither Black nor White, there is neither Hispanic nor Asian, there is neither Baptist nor Methodist. If Paul could see the Christian church today and the segregation that exists within it, would he still say that "we are all one in Christ Jesus?" The answer is yes, because the truth does not change. Moreover, because the truth is what gives us freedom, I believe that Paul would want to deal with this great teacher of the faith in this 21st century. I think that Paul would want to tear down the walls of resistance that stop the God-given message of salvation given to us through the death and resurrection of Jesus Christ from reaching across cultural lines. However, I do not believe that Paul's strategy in doing this would be to try and convince people that they are color-blind.

I think that Paul would want us to recognize our differences, rather than try to cover them up. I believe that Paul would encourage us to focus on the Gospel of reconciliation and remind people that different does not mean deficient. We may be different, but we are still one in Christ Jesus. According to James Nieman and Thomas Rogers, in their book, *Preaching to Every Pew: Cross-Cultural Strategies*:

> The Church has always been understood as a community whose members are fundamentally

different from one another. The apostle Paul describes the church using the image of the human body composed of parts as different as hands, feet, and eyes (I Corinthians 12:12-26). In so doing, Paul argues for the necessity of such differences. The hand is not a foot, and we would be in trouble if it were. Moreover, this body metaphor connects our differences to Christ. If we take seriously the one we claim as Lord, we must expect and embrace diversities. It is necessary for members to be different for the church to be the body of Christ in and for the world... The goal has never been to homogenize the people of God but to move to a greater mutual understanding and appreciation of our differences... To embrace the theological depth of human diversity can free us to rejoice in those differences whose unity is found in being joined together in Christ.[44]

Therefore, although we may be different, separated and divided, because of the love of the Triune God, we can be reconciled to God and one another. It would benefit us to embrace our theological differences so that we might find ourselves joined together in Christ not only in word, but indeed. If we as servants of the Most High, God want to gain a hearing and overcome the resistances we face, this is the message we must preach.

---

[44]James Nieman and Thomas G. Rogers, *Preaching to Every Pew: Cross-Cultural Strategies.* (Minneapolis: Fortress Press, 2001.) p. 142

There is a strategy to preaching this word in various cultures. Because I believe most Black preaching is rhetorical, in order to explain this point, I focused on the rhetorical strategies Paul used in Athens, as recorded in Acts Chapter Seventeen. Paul's purpose for going to Athens was to win souls for Christ. When he arrived and saw the city was full of idols, it broke his heart. The city was still recognized as a center of culture and education, but it had lost its political glory. While the famous university and the fine buildings were still structurally present, the city was not as influential as it once was. In Acts 17, Paul's work in Athens begins with him speaking in the synagogue with the Jews and witnessing in the marketplace to the Greeks.

When the Council of the Areopagus heard about Paul's teaching, the members invited him to present his teaching before the council on Mars' Hill. Here is where Paul puts his rhetorical strategy to work. Marion L. Soards says, it is through "building on the unknown that Paul declares his intentions."[45] I see him doing at least four things in this situation. First, he mentions the altar of the "unknown god." Secondly, he explains who the unknown god is. Thirdly, he describes the attributes of the unknown God. Finally, after arousing their

---

[45]Marion L. Soards, *The Speeches in Acts: Their Content, Context and Concern*, (Louisville, Westminster John Knox, 1994), p.97

attention, he challenges the council to consider the moral issues before them.

Paul's strategy in engaging the people of Athens is brilliant. First, he went into the city, observed what was around him, studied the people, read their literature and engaged them in conversation. As he looked the city over, one of the things he observed was an altar that was dedicated to an unknown god. In speaking to the council, the first thing he does is compliment the piety of the people in Athens, recorded in Acts17:22. He then uses the statue of the unknown God as his focal point of what this group of unbelievers already knew about God, and then by using their own logic and philosophy he led them to what they needed to learn about God. In Acts 17:23, he says "Now what you worship as something unknown I am going to proclaim to you."

Paul realized there was a revealed knowledge of God that existed among the people, so he started his message by referring to this revealed knowledge and telling the Athenians that this is the God he proclaims. Soards says, this "leads to a series of statements about God, about both God's character, and God dealing with humanity strongly indicating God's authority."[46] Next, Paul tells the Council they have a misinterpreted understanding of God. From this point on, he

---

[46]Ibid. p. 97

jumps back and forth between what the Athenians know and what they need to know about God. This rhetorical strategy is both brilliant and problematic. Its brilliance is seen in the fact that Paul uses it to defend his proclamation against charges of presenting a foreign God. However, it is problematic because he uses fiction to make them believe their piety is logically valid. This is an unacceptable idea to a true worshiper of God.

Paul's rhetorical strategy continues with the following themes: the importance of God, the goodness of God, the authority of God, and the grace of God. From verse 25-29 Paul ends with what his listeners needed to know about God, by explaining to this group of Athenians some of the attributes of the true God. He tells them that the true God does not need people to sustain him, rather he sustains all things; participates in human existence; and made us in His image. He then points out to them that what they are doing is called idolatry and that idolatry is illogical. The worship of an image is not logical because how can a God who created people be an image or an idol? Paul's mission is to convince the Athenians to repent of their sins and turn in faith to Christ. Even so, he knows their ignorance will hinder their ability to have a relationship with God, so he encourages them to have faith in God.

Paul's final strategy introduces the Athenians to the concept of repentance, judgment, and resurrection. Although

Paul was very crafty and rhetorical in his presentation, some of the Athenians did not want to hear this talk of resurrection. The concept that Paul presents here is that all people will be raised from the dead, just as Jesus was. This is more than most of them can accept as good news. Up to this point he had no problems from his listeners, but at this point his speech is interrupted, and the people divide into three parts: those who mock his message, those who want to hear more of the message, and those who believe and follow.

This is a very good rhetorical sermon that conveys the ultimate truth about God. Here, Paul took the opportunity to tell the Athenians that although they were religious, they were ignorant. Then, to relieve them of their ignorance, he introduced them to the true and living God. After sharing the truth with them, he tells them the time for ignorance is over. God has sent a Man whom he raised from the dead, and now is the day of repentance, for the Day of Judgment is coming. In other words, Paul laid out the order of things in this manner: ignorance, revelation, knowledge, declaration, repentance and judgment. He said, in essence, that the way to avoid judgment was to acknowledge where they were in that sequence of events and make a decision to accept God's grace.

Anticipated Resistance

This kind of preaching will always stir up resistance, so I thought about what kind of resistances I have encountered. In my thirty-four years of preaching, I have learned every church has its own unique culture. Sometimes what the preacher intends to say may not connect theologically or Biblically with those who hear the message, especially if the preacher does not know anything about the storyline of the church.

Resistance #1 - So, one resistance I sought to avoid was that of going against the theological culture of the church. I think it is important for a preacher to know what theology is being preached in the church before he/she prepares the sermon. For example, if the storyline of the church includes the principle of tithing, and a guest preacher comes in and preaches against tithing, this might be confusing to the hearers. If the pastor of the church is preaching about faith by works, and the guest preacher preaches a message about works by faith, this may confuse the hearers and cause some resistance if it is not clarified. The resistance to overcome in this case is the resistance to change. Some people just do not care for change, so when change is presented in a manner that is not enticing, some listeners will automatically go into a defensive mode and shut the preacher out.

Resistance #2 - The second resistance I thought I should be aware of was that of Biblical literacy. If I wanted to gain a hearing by the various congregations to whom I would be preaching, I needed to be sure they understood the language I used when explaining the text. Words can mean different things in diverse cultures. For example, in my culture, if I said, "the woman couldn't straighten herself up," that could easily be interpreted to mean she needed help straighten up her spiritual life. In another culture it could simply mean she had a physical condition that needed healing. To avoid that kind of resistance when making such statements, I needed to be sure to define what I meant. Realizing that I probably would be preaching to a congregation that had a different lifestyle and mindset than my usual audience, to avoid the resistance of irrelevance, I knew I needed to understand their values, pursuits, griefs and anxieties.

Resistance #3 - Often as preachers we tend to focus on what we will preach without giving any thought at all about to whom we will be preaching. The resistance to gaining a hearing here comes in the fact that not many people want to hear a message that does not relate to them in one way or another. Thus, during these four weeks I also read as much as I could about the church and about the city in which the church was located. If the church had a webpage, I viewed the information listed on the page. This information helped me to understand how the church viewed family, education, mission work and more. In my opinion, preaching should touch the hearts of the hearers with a heartfelt message from God.

Resistance #4 -Another resistance that one might face in preaching in a different culture would be the resistance of fear, doubt and uncertainty. The resistance to gaining a hearing here is in being able to convince the people that the word you preach is a Word from God. This is a very self-sacrificing and fear-provoking task. To overcome this resistance, it is important that the preacher makes sure the message is both relevant and practical.

Resistance #5 - Sometimes the preacher cannot gain a hearing from the congregation simply because of his/her style of preaching. When I say "style," I am not necessarily talking about the delivery of the sermon. It has been my experience that some congregations like topical sermons, some like meta-narrative sermons, and others like expository sermons, to name a few styles. In my cultural context, in what we call silk stocking churches, the audiences like a soft-toned type of message and worship. In other words, they do not like noises, shouts, and a lot of moving around. In the more charismatic churches, hard-toned types of messages are preferred. In other words, audiences want the preacher to whoop, holler, jump, stomp, walk or whatever it takes to hold their attention and to demonstrate the message physically. In order to overcome the resistance to gaining a hearing, the preacher needs to know something about the way the people hear a sermon. If the pastor of the church has recorded sermons available online, these can be of great aid in overcoming the resistance to the style of preaching.

Because I am very accustomed to hearing Black sermons preached in a circular and emotional form, when preaching to Black congregations, instead of being just instructive, my preaching tends to be more emotional and uplifting. In other words, to express the importance of a point in the sermon, I will often state a point, relate the point to some cultural issue or problem, state the point again and continue the cycle until I feel the point has been clearly made. Then, I will end the sermon with a high cultural climactic style of preaching known as "call and response." However, in many cultures, the call and response style of preaching is often misjudged and spoken of by others as being too emotional, unnecessary and non-logical.

In talking about Black preaching, C. F. Stewart writes, "Not only did words quicken responses from the audience, but the process of call and response itself has ritual significance in simulating unity and solidarity among people whose basic strength is in unified belief and action."[47] Contrary to popular belief, call and response is not only about getting the audience involved. Experience has proven that when preaching to a people that have been oppressed and who may have to face large hurdles every day of their lives, logic alone may not be enough to get the message across. Therefore, along with logic and information, the Black preacher often uses techniques such as facial expressions, hand gestures, props, call and response and much more to assure the message will be received by the listeners.

In explaining the role of these preaching strategies, Stewart offers the following example of call and response as an indication of its primary role in socialization:

Speaker:	And there will come a time when we will see another day.
Audience:	That's right. We will!
Speaker:	And nobody will turn us 'round when that day comes!
Audience:	That's right, say it!
Speaker:	Whatever we want to say, we got to say that God is in charge of this thing and can nor person, mind, nor mule stand in God's way when god decides to do something!
Audience:	You know you right. That's right. Go 'head. Say it!
Speaker:	So, let's stand up and take action! Let's stand up to those

---

[47]Stewart, C. F., *Soul Survivors:* 66.

	drug dealers and run them out of town because this is God's place and we are God's people. If we take two steps, God will take ten on our behalf!"
Audience:	That's it! Let's do it! Let's go. God is with us![48]

The purpose of this call and response was to make the congregation aware of a social issue, to encourage and motivate them into action. Thus, while the preaching method of call and response can be very emotional, it can also be very logical and informative.

However, when employing a call and response style of preaching, one must constantly be reminded of the fact that substance is more important than form. While the skillful use of the preacher's hands, eye contact and body language are important to preaching, it must be enhanced by the use of substance. So, another thing I have learned about my preaching through my Book is that while style is important, the preacher must have some substance behind his or her method or technique in order for preaching to be effective. Though there are some similarities between performance and preaching, style should not become a substitute for substance. Instead, it should become the vehicle for expressing the substance.

---

[48]Ibid.

After reading Brosend's book, I now understand that dialogical preaching is not as much about understanding the text, as it is about being responsive to the "concerns, questions, needs, and hopes" of the congregation. In my opinion, if the preacher does not both hear and connect the Word of God to the listeners' needs, he/she has not preached the Word of God. John Neuhaus in his book, *Freedom for Ministry* writes,

> Preaching and hearing goes together. A person listening is vital to good preaching because the pulpit and pew are engaged in a common work. Nowhere is this more evident than in the black church where the people are actually helping the preacher to preach.[49]

When Neuhaus writes that the people are helping the preacher preach, he is referring to what is called Black preaching. In Black preaching there is a connection between the preacher and the listener that is called "call and response." Here I would like to revisit this strategy from a unique perspective.

Call and response in this perspective is a method of preaching in which the listeners let the preacher know they understand the point he/she is making. Most of the time, this affirmation comes by means of an oral response. If the

---

[49]John Neuhaus, *Freedom of Ministry* (Grand Rapids, MI: Eerdmans, 1979) p.175

preacher makes a point that applies to an individual's life or circumstance, an affirmation of some kind is given orally. This lets the preacher know the message has been accepted and applied to the lives of the listeners. Another benefit of the call and response type preaching is the congregation's response says to a preacher, thank you for caring enough to make this sermon relevant to my life.

When a preacher has worked hard and preached hard, he/she expects for the congregation to let him/her know that his/her labor was not in vain. Some people call this preaching for a shout, because if there is no response, many Black preachers feel their message has failed. In other words, if there is no response to the preached word, the preacher may leave from the preaching moment disappointed. But if there is a response, the preacher comes away with a sense of accomplishment. This kind of response is so important to some preachers that if they do not get an immediate response, some will pause and wait for one. In some cases, they will say things in the sermon like, "Y'all don't hear me!" or "I wish I had somebody!" or "Can I get a witness?"

Stewart states, "Call and response affirms each other's presence. The notion of collective unity in the midst of diversity is exemplified."[50] In this dialogical setting, it is

---

[50]C. F. Stewart, *Soul Survivors*: p. 65.

assumed that the Holy Spirit shows up and the people participate in the preaching with chanted responses such as: "Say that Preacher, preach!," "Praise the Lord!," "Show you right!," and "Amen, Sister!" When this happens, the preacher is given a sense that a connection is being made between the preacher and the listeners, which says that God is responding to the needs of the people. When the preacher experiences this affirmation, he/she knows the purpose of the sermon has been accomplished.

In my cultural experience, preaching is a survival instrument. Most people to whom I preach come to church to hear a word that will inspire and restore hope in lives that are filled with reasons to be hopeless and separated from the world of success. To these people, the emotional energy exhibited in most Black preaching grants the listener an assurance of grace found only in the love of Jesus Christ. For this to happen, the preacher and the congregation must both understand and experience the sermon. The hearers experience this grace by relating the problem to their own lives. Then, after the problem has been introduced, the sermon shows how the Word of God can be used to solve the problem. Once listeners have experienced the sermon, they may shout, run or cry or wave their hands in the air. This is called celebration and comes when the celebrant realizes that a connection between their problem and the Biblical text reveals a way out of their unfavorable situation.

Frank A. Thomas writes in his book, *They Like to Never Quit Praisin' God,* "the one who preaches is expected to say the 'right thing rightly.'"[51] To say the right thing rightly requires more than quoting the scripture. Thus, in order to preach this word, the first strategy we must possess is the ability to not only correctly teach the Word of God, but to correctly apply it. I have discovered some strategies I believe will help me develop my preaching in a cross-cultural setting.

Strategy for Gaining a Hearing

Strategy #1 - If I am to be a good cross-cultural preacher, I must learn to study the needs of my audience's culture and minister to them from the scriptures. I must actively connect with the audience by involving myself in their everyday activities. In other words, by working, visiting, and studying the culture of others, they will feel that I really want to become one of them. This assurance helps the preacher to gain deeper credibility in the eyes of his/her audiences. In doing this,

[51]Frank A. Thomas, *They Like to Never Quit Praisin' God* (Cleveland; The Pilgrim Press,1997) p. 12

I must not seek to make other cultures think like my culture, but because each culture has its own communication styles, I must learn to communicate in ways the people will understand and accept.

Strategy #2 - Another stratagem that I feel needs to take place to gain a hearing in various cultural contexts is that the pulpit authority must be restored. In most of the interviews that I conducted, the conversation was really more about administration than it was about preaching. It seems that more people have a concern about who leads them than they do about who preaches to them. It's almost like peoples' response to preaching is we can take it, or we can leave it. Our preaching is just a speech that anyone can perform; the source of the speech doesn't really matter from. In the A.M.E. Church, the pulpit podium is placed in the center of the stage as a symbol of the sacredness and power of the words that are spoken it. When I first started to preach, no one could mount the pulpit podium except for the one who had been called to preach. Even then, it was at the pastor's discretion as to whether or not you could preach from their podium.

In other words, in many churches, only the pastor and the pastor's invited guest are allowed to preach from the pulpit podium. If the pastor of the church does not invite you to speak from the pulpit, then you are to speak from a smaller podium on the floor. In some of the churches I have preached outside of my cultural context, the pulpit area and podium have no sacredness whatsoever. Everyone who speaks enters the pulpit and makes their address from the podium. From selling Girl Scout cookies to raffling off a chance to win a pig, I have seen the message go forth from the pulpit podium. This change relating to the authority of where the preached word is proclaimed may be a part of the reason why many in America have lost touch with the power of the Word of God.

In many churches today, if you are female, you will not preach from the pulpit podium. I can accept and respect that because it is consistent with what they teach based on their interpretation of the Pauline texts. I can also accept that, because it is in that space that they have been called and from that space they must be able to feel the sacredness and presence of God. What I think sometimes hinders the hearing of the Word of God is that many pastors have relinquished the sacredness of the pulpit that once gave inspiration to the hearing of the preached word. Some have gone as far as even to remove the pulpit podium from the pulpit. I understand the reasoning behind this is that many preachers are moving toward dialogical preaching strategies, where there is a conversation between the preacher and the congregation during the sermon. While I am not criticizing this style of preaching, I do believe that there may have been more lost in this move than was gained. While some churches discriminate against women in the pulpit, many Black churches still refuse to allow anyone behind the sacred desk who has not been ordained to preach the Word of God. I do not know if bringing back the authority of the place where the word is proclaimed will help women gain a hearing in various cultural counters, but I do believe it is worth the try.

Strategy #3 - Another strategy that I believe is important in gaining a hearing in various cultural contexts is the strategy of preaching for results. I find that many times when preachers stand behind the sacred desk they are not focusing on getting a result or a response to the message. The purpose of their preaching is to fill in the part of the order of worship that calls for a sermon. In contrast, Christ-centered preaching should have the purpose of moving someone to accept the message and to give their lives to the service of the Kingdom of God. I feel that rather than being surprised when someone gives their life to Christ and joins the church, we should be disappointed when no one does. If there are unsaved people in the audience, we should expect the Holy Spirit to convict them. If a preacher prepares a Christ-centered message with an intent to call, to convert and to compel the hearer into some action based on the message, chances are that someone will hear and make a commitment to accept the invitation. But, if we preach with expectation of getting nothing, nothing will probably be what we get. If the invitation is not offered, many will leave uncommitted even if they feel the call of God on their lives. Preaching must have a purpose if it is to be heard in any cultural context.

Strategy #4 - Another strategy is to take time to investigate the ways that the audience may be motivated. In some cultures, motivations are left up to the choice of the individual. In other words, what he/she will do with his/her time, efforts, choice of life partner, money, occupation and beliefs is left to each person to decide. In this setting, the preacher must learn to adapt his or her message to fit what will motivate the audience. This can be done by examining the social structures of the audiences' culture. This will include learning something about their educational levels, ranks, statuses, and positions on social issues. Because the goal of some cultures is to please their ancestors, a good preacher will spend time learning how to accentuate the positive without condemning the negative parts of the audience's culture. They will try to learn the language of the audience's culture and communicate with symbols, objects, and stories that are familiar to the people. If we are to gain a hearing in various cultural contexts, we must learn the spiritual means of interpreting truth, and the best ways of illustrating and applying this truth in a culture.

This Project practicum has revealed the following findings:

Finding #1 - The first person that I interviewed believes in preaching the doctrines of the church. By doctrines of the church, I refer to the theological beliefs of the church such as the doctrine of God, Jesus, the Holy Spirit, etc. For more information on these doctrines, refer to chapter one of this book.

My first interviewee is very well educated, theologically sound and very well versed in the Scriptures. Her testimony is that she has no problem gaining a hearing even though she preaches in a culture that is outside of her own. Her strategy is to take sympathetic beliefs of the church and help other people understand how these doctrines can help them deal with the issues that they face in the world. Our conversation revealed that a good doctrinal sermon will clearly define, describe and apply the doctrine to the practical uses the doctrine makes in the lives of the hearers. Carl Williams defines doctrinal preaching as "Christian preaching grounded in the biblical witness to Jesus Christ; it starts with text, doctrine, or cultural question, but tends to focus on one or more Christian doctrines regardless of its starting point."[52]

---

[52]William J. Carl III. *Preaching Christian Doctrine*, (Philadelphia: Fortress Press, 1984) p.8-9

In order for the doctrine to express hope to hurting people, the hearers must be able to interpret the doctrinal sermon in light of Christ's perspective on life. In other words, preaching doctrine is important as long as the doctrine is made relevant to the lives of those who hear. If the preacher disregards the importance of the relevance of the doctrine, the sermon runs the risk of being too theoretical and too hard for the hearers to understand. However, in sharing the revealers of the doctrine, one must also be careful not to force the doctrine on people by threatening them. Making statements like, "If you don't believe this, then this will happen," can be more harmful than helpful. A better way of getting people to accept the doctrine is to relate the doctrine to the love of Christ rather than to the consequences of not accepting the doctrine. For an experiential preacher like me, it is important that the doctrine is preached not just to inform, but to change, transform, touch and relate to people in their daily lives.

For this reason, many experiential preachers are tempted to dispense with preaching the doctrines of the church. This project practicum revealed that this is an area in which I need much improvement. The Bible tells us in 2 Timothy 4:2-3 that there will come a time when people will not listen to sound doctrine. Timothy George writes that "the recovery of doctrinal preaching is essential to the renewal of the church." [53]I am now aware of the fact that preaching is not a matter of whether to preach doctrine and theological sermons or not, it is a matter of preaching them in a way that the hearers realize why the doctrine matters. As with any sermon, a sermon that preaches doctrine must have good planning. Without good preparation, we will end up being repetitive in our teaching of the doctrine. Unprepared sermons make for boring sermons. Therefore, when preaching doctrinal sermons, the preacher should make sure first of all that the doctrine has touched his/her heart. If the preacher is interested in what the Gospel is saying about the doctrine, then the preacher can get excited about presenting it to others.

It takes hard work to preach doctrinal sermons, but a good way to begin is to ask how the sermon applies to the daily lives of the people who will hear it preached. As I wrote earlier in this book, there is a difference between a Biblical sermon and a Biblical lecture. The purpose of a Biblical lecture is to inform the hearers of Biblical facts, but the purpose of a sermon should be transformation. The sermon should move the hearers from where they are into an encounter with God, who can heal, save, guide and provide hope to them. Because an encounter with God changes people, the preacher should have

---

[53]Timothy George, "Doctrinal Preaching", in the Handbook of Contemporary Preaching, Michael Duduit, ed., (Nashville: Broadman Press, 1993) p.93.

an expectation of some kind of positive response from the hearers. Thus, in order to gain a hearing when preaching doctrinal sermons, there needs to be a connection between the preacher, the message, the hearers and God. Moreover, when preaching doctrinal sermons in various cultural contexts, if it is to be heard, the sermon must be elucidating the importance of the doctrine so that there is a connection between doctrine, experience of humanity and Christ.

Finding #2 – While the third person I interviewed was quite radical in her views of the Black church, she was right about expository preaching. "Expository preaching," she said, "is the fundamental method of properly exegeting the Word of God. It is what is needed to help the preacher keep the focus on God through Jesus Christ and to keep her focus off of self-centered man." Robert Thomas defines exegesis as "the critical or technical application of hermeneutical principles to a biblical text in the original languages with a view to the exposition or declaration of its meaning."[54] Whereas there are probably as many styles of preaching as there are preachers, in my opinion the best way to gain a hearing of a Christ-centered message is through expository preaching. If the scriptural texts have been accurately exegeted and the message addresses the needs of the congregation, the preacher's style of preaching is

---

[54]Robert L. Thomas, *Introduction to Exegesis* (Sun Valley: author, 1987) 15-16.

really not important. Rather, what is important is that the Word of God is accurately exegeted and effectually communicated.

According to Robert L. Thomas in an article entitled, "The Relationship between Exegesis and Expository Preaching," he writes:

> The distinctive characteristic of expository preaching is its instructional function. An explanation of the details of a given text imparts information that is otherwise unavailable to the average untrained parishioner and provides him with a foundation for Christian growth and service. The importance and centrality of thorough exegesis in preparing the expositor for this service cannot be overstated. Exegesis must itself be on a solid footing and must lead to development in supplementary fields that, in turn, provide important data for expository preaching, too. With the raw material of sermon preparation thus obtained, common-sense principles must be applied in putting the material into a form that the congregation can receive with ease and learn from.[55]

---

[55]Robert L. Thomas, "Bible Translations: The Link between Exegesis and Expository Preaching" The Master's Seminary Journal 1/1 (Spring 1990) 53.

I believe that if a preacher combines this strategy of expository preaching with properly exegeting text and addressing the needs of the hearers, then she may gain a hearing in any cultural context. I believe it is obvious that exegesis and expository preaching work together to bring about a clear word from the Lord, but the question is, how does one convince a preacher of the importance of this strategy? Far too many preachers rely solely on the power of the Holy Spirit to do the work God called us to do.

Now, I believe in the power of the Holy Spirit. In fact, the only way we can move from the exegesis to the sermon preparation to the delivery of the word is by the power of the Holy Spirit. But I also believe that before the Holy Spirit can work in the lives of the hearers, the Holy Spirit must have already been at work in the life of the preacher. 1Thessalonians 1:4-5 reads," For we know, brothers and sisters loved by God, that he has chosen you, because our gospel came to you not simply with words but also with power, with the Holy Spirit and deep conviction." Thus, I believe the only way for preachers to achieve the work God calls us to do through preaching is that we first must receive the Gospel ourselves. Again, I refer to Bishop Vashti McKenzie's statement: "The message must be biblically based and rooted in the preacher's relationship with God and the preacher's connection with the Holy Spirit."[56]

Some preachers think that reading the text and standing to preach without any preparation other than prayer and personal analysis is all that we need. This is the reason many of our sermons are called "nice little speeches" or great little talks. Some preachers think that all they need to do is to combine a story or two with a scriptural text and that ought to be enough to make people's lives acceptable to God. I do not agree. The Bible tells us in Hebrews 4:12 that, "The word of God is alive and active. Sharper than any double-edged sword, it penetrates even to dividing soul and spirit, joints and marrow; it judges the thoughts and attitudes of the heart." If the Word of God is preached in a way that people can understand, using language that people can relate to, and focusing on the hearts and minds of the believers, then yes, a hearing of this word can be gained in various cultural contexts. Otherwise, I would say the answer is no. Philosopher Anthony Thiselton informs us that:

> Hermeneutics is a circular process and human prejudgments make objective interpretation impossible. At best it has

---

[56]McKenzie, Ibid. see reference 20 of this paper.

the effect of destroying the goal of
objectivity that traditional Protestant
interpretation has always pursued, and
at worst it signals an end of rationality
in studying the Bible.[57]

---

[57]Anthony C. Thiselton, "The Two Horizons" (Grand Rapids: Eerdmans,
1980) 105, 110; idem, "The New Hermeneutic," in New Testament
Interpretation (I. Howard Marshall, ed.; Grand Rapids Eerdmans, 1977) p.
317.

In other words,
in order to gain a hearing
that will change
lives and save souls
in any culture,
the truth of the Word of God
must be properly prepared,
rightly divided,
purposefully
delivered and faithfully
preached.

~~~✝ ~~~✝ ~~~✝ ~~~

Conclusion

This Book has made me realize that there are three things that I cannot change. Those three things are the fact that I am Black, I am a woman, and I am a preacher. One might argue that I could be seen as a lecturer, a teacher, or a motivational speaker, but that argument would be incorrect. I am a preacher. When I say I am a preacher, I mean that I have the spiritual gift of preaching. One of the reasons I say I am a preacher and not a lecturer is because of the great desire burning within my heart to reach both the believer and the unbeliever with a Christ-centered, life-changing word. While I admit that there is some overlapping of teaching and motivational speaking in my preaching, that is not who I am. Preaching is what I do, because of who I am. I did not choose to be born Black, and I did not choose to be born a female, and I did not choose to be called to preach; therefore, I cannot choose to undo any of these three distinguishing features of my life. I am a preacher because the message I preach is delivered with a desire to provide the hearers with hope, healing, deliverance and salvation, as well as direction and information.

Unlike a speech or a lecture, which points to itself, a sermon points to God. An experiential Christ-centered sermon has the ability to be informative, interactive and transformative. This transformation takes place in the lives of the hearers when the message points towards God rather than humanity. In other words, when the hearers are given a more accurate picture of God, lives are changed. I have an intense need to tell others about the life, death and resurrection of Jesus Christ, not just for the sake of information, knowledge or motivation, but to elicit a response that leads those who hear my message into an encounter with God. Therefore, when my message is called "a little talk" or "a nice speech," the purpose is denigrated. This Project has shown me that such encounters with God can only happen through Christ-centered preaching that is related to the experience of the hearers.

The question this Book seeks to answer is this: How can an experiential, emotional approach to preaching that traditionally has been a vital component of the Black preaching style be combined with a more conceptual, linear approach to preaching to maximize the effectiveness of sermons preached by Black Females in and beyond their own cultural contexts? While I still think that is a good question to ponder, what I have discovered through this Project practicum is that when a person has been given the gift of preaching, she/he rarely thinks about such things as style and presentation. Instead, the preacher's preparation usually concentrates on the substance and power of the Word of God to bring about the desired results. A dependency on one's faith in God, the passionate desire of one's heart and the anointing of God's Holy Spirit takes priority over style and presentation. Because of this dependency on God, preaching strategies are often overlooked. So, I began this final chapter by saying that this project practicum has afforded me a rare but useful opportunity to observe my approach to preaching as well as my identity as a preacher.

Another reason that I say that I am a preacher and not a lecturer is because, as an ex-schoolteacher, I understand that the purpose of a lecture is to prepare people to take tests or exams on the presented subject. At best, the function of a lecture is to transfer information. Even if the information is conveyed in such a manner that the hearer receives it, unless it points to the redeeming power of God, the only relationship that can be built is between the hearer, the lesson and the speaker. Usually lectures will only point to information. I am not saying that information is unimportant, but I am saying no matter how eloquent or how emotional a lecture is, it is informational only and will most likely not be viewed as a message from God.

Preaching, on the other hand, is not meant to prepare a person to take an exam or to write a paper about God; rather, it is meant to prepare a person to experience the glory of God. Of course, a portion of that message will relate the character (ethos) of the preacher, but usually when a Christ-centered message is preached, and the hearers feel a movement of God's Holy Spirit (pathos), all involved become overwhelmed by the glory of God (logos), not humanity. As a preacher this is the kind of response I seek from the preached word. I seek responses that indicate a desire to be saved, or to gain knowledge of God's presence in hurtful or painful situations, or to gain a desire to live a more devoted or committed Christian life.

It is obvious from the evaluations of my preaching, that I am very well-liked, and that people enjoy my preaching. However, I contend that that should not be the purpose for preaching. If the only reason the preacher preaches is for the pleasure of the listener, then they have missed the purpose of their calling. The evaluation of a sermon should not be based upon whether a person thinks the sermon sounds or feels good. In accordance with the words of Frank Thomas, as I quoted earlier, who said that we should say the "right thing rightly,"[58] I also believe that we should do the right thing for the right reason. In other words, sometimes when a person says that a sermon is good, they may be right, but they are right for the wrong reason. In their opinion a good sermon may be defined as a sermon that is well exegeted, theologically sound, doctrinally true, emotionally experienced, and passionately

---

[58]Ibid. Frank Thomas

delivered. But if that is the reason the sermon was prepared; the sermon may be good but for the wrong reason.

So, can an experiential emotional approach to preaching be combined with a conceptual linear approach to preaching to maximize the effect of sermons preached by Black females in various cultural contexts? This is still a good question, as long as the focus is placed on the phrase "maximize the effect of sermons." The relevance of the question is not in the preaching style or the approach to preaching, but in the importance of the purpose of preaching. The purpose of preaching is something that we do not think about correctly. This is one of the most disturbing things I realized during this Project. I interviewed three outstanding women preachers, preached five well-prepared messages and conversed with six very intelligent and outstanding women who love The Lord and who are inspired by my preaching. But at the close of the day I had to ask myself, what was my purpose in doing this Project? The disturbing thing that I discovered was that while I had several reasons for doing this Project, I had not considered my purpose.

My reason was to investigate strategies and provide insights into what I was already doing as a Black female preacher who preaches across cultural lines, to prepare other Black females to experience the same ministry opportunities and benefits. Maybe I should have called this Project "Doing the Right Thing for the Wrong Reasons," because in reality God does not need Black females to do what I am doing. God already has me. What God needs is for us to do what we are called to do with the purpose God has intended. So, the question remains, what is the purpose? For what purpose has God permitted me the opportunity to preach across cultural lines? I believe God wants me to share all the strategies and insights that I have gained during this Project, but I also believe that a failure to consider the purpose of why the strategies are important could be devastating.

This Book has talked about Christ-centered preaching, it has talked about doctrinal preaching, it has talked about expository preaching, it has talked about Black preaching, it has talked about dialogical preaching, and it has talked about experiential and conceptual approaches to preaching, but it has not addressed what God would have the preacher do. As agents of God's communication, we are not called just to be creative and practical about preaching, we are called to have a passion about God's propose for preaching. So, I conclude that the most important insight and strategy that a preacher needs in order to overcome resistances to gaining a hearing in various cultural contexts is a heart that burns for the Lord.

If I would do this Project again, part of my Book would be focused on teaching other women about my passion, love, and desire for the call of God on my life. Why are so many attracted to my preaching? I believe it is not that they are attracted to me or my preaching style; rather, it is that they are attracted to the passion I have for the God that calls me. This passion I have for God is the root of my purpose for laboring in mental (logos), emotional (pathos) and personal (ethos) preparation for preaching the Word of God. In other words, my purpose is to persuade others of the importance of loving God, body, soul and mind. Michael Fabarez, in his book, *Preaching that Changes Lives*, argues that the correct evaluation of an effective sermon is "the biblical change it brings about in the lives of our congregants."[59] I believe that is a good explanation of our purpose for preaching. Our purpose should be to gain a hearing that will bring about a change in the lives of the congregants. Our purpose for having a good theology of preaching is to emphasize the effects of that theology.

My Book talks a lot about the method of preaching, but I think that I fail in many areas to emphasize the purpose of preaching. I tried to make it plain that preaching is not just about lecturing or giving information, but that preaching is about bringing about a transformation in the lives of the

---

[59]Michael Fabarez, *Preaching that Changes Lives* (Eugene, OR: Wipf and Stock Publishers, 2002), 9-10.

hearers. However, I think preaching is about even more than that. The purpose of preaching is not just combining an explanation of the Word of God with the application of that Word. The purpose of preaching, I believe, is best explained by R. Albert Mohler, Jr in his book, *A Theology of Preaching, Handbook of Contemporary Preaching*.

> He writes "True preaching begins with this confession: we preach because God has spoken."[60] Now, that is powerful! Our purpose for preaching is the fact that God has spoken and has called us to reveal what God has said. This is probably the most important insight for any preacher who wants to gain a hearing in any cultural context. As an agent of God's communication, our purpose for preaching should be grounded on the foundational truth and persuasion of the fact that God has spoken. God has spoken and has given us a mouth full of words called the Gospel of Jesus Christ, and as agents of God's communication we have been called, commissioned and compelled to preach this Gospel.

---

[60]R. Albert Mohler, Jr., *"A Theology of Preaching,"* Handbook of *Contemporary Preaching,* Michael Duduitt, ed., (Nashville: Broadman Press, 1992), 14.

This good news is not just for the hearers of the preached word, but also for the one who preaches this Gospel. The good news for those of us who have found our purpose in preaching is that the same God who saves through the preaching of the Word has also promised to send us the power to preach effectively through the Holy Spirit. The Holy Spirit, not our intellect or articulation or personality, is the one who validates the purpose of the preachers called. The purpose of preaching is for the preacher to accomplish God's purpose by the revelation of God's spoken word and to bring glory to God in the process. The good news for those of us who have been called to be agents of God's communication is that God still uses human preachers to accomplish this task. Therefore, if the preacher learns the strategy of preparing sermons that both glorify God and reveal God's glory to both the saved and the lost, we shall gain a hearing of the spoken word no matter where we stand to preach.

Thus, my concluding statement for this Book is that in order to gain a hearing and to overcome the resistances one faces in gaining that hearing, the preacher must remain faithful to the calling of revealing what God has spoken in the Holy Bible. This is what we have been called to do, to express God's glory in and beyond our cultural context. God has not only called us to be agents of God's communication, but God has commanded us to preach. We are not called to defend whether or not God has called us to preach in or out of our cultural context. We must be persuaded ourselves, but we do not have to prove it to others. Why God chose to call us to preach is a mystery that I cannot answer. But, one thing I know is that the call of God on our lives has come so that we may defend the faith! In other words, we have not been called to defend preaching, we have been called to defend the faith through the preaching of the life, death, resurrection and return of Christ.

Therefore, the number one sermonic strategy a preacher must have in order to overcome the resistances to gaining a hearing in and beyond our cultural contexts is simply this: Preach!

> In the presence of God and of Christ Jesus, who will judge the living and the dead, and in view of his appearing and his kingdom, I give you this charge: Preach the word; be prepared in season and out of season; correct, rebuke and encourage—with great patience and careful instruction. For, the time will come when people will not put up with sound doctrine. Instead, to suit their own desires, they will gather around them a substantial number of teachers to say what their itching ears want to hear. They will turn their ears away from the truth and turn aside to myths. But you, keep your head in all situations, endure hardship, do the work of an evangelist, and discharge all the duties of your ministry. Timothy 4:1-5.

For, the time will come when people will not put up with sound doctrine. Instead, to suit their own desires, they will gather around them a substantial number of teachers to say what their itching ears want to hear. The will turn their ears away from the truth and turn aside to myths.

APPENDICES

Appendix One – Exegesis

Congregational exegesis of text - Each bullet point was the result of the congregation's insight and discussion of the text.

The woman that was bent
- The woman was given no name in this text.
- The woman had an eighteen-year illness.
- Her condition was described as being bound to Satan.
- The result of her condition was she could not stand up straight
- She could not look anyone in the eyes
- She had problems with her everyday social relationships.
- In spite of these conditions, the woman walks into church.
- Because she was in church on the right day, she encountered Jesus, who saw her, called her and touched her.
- When Jesus touched her, she was healed. After the woman was healed, her response was to praise God.
- The woman came to church to worship.
- She did not come for healing; therefore, she did not approach Jesus, nor did she request to be healed.
- There is no mention in this text of the woman's faith.
- It was mentioned that she was a daughter of Abraham.
- It was also mentioned that her sickness was a result of bondage.
- She had a bondage that came from Satan.

- And Jesus declared that she should be free from that bondage.

A view of Jesus from this text
- Jesus was in church on the Sabbath Day.
- As was his custom he was teaching in the synagogue.
- He saw the woman
- He called her, and he touched her, and she was healed by his touch. There is no mention of prayer in this text. There was no time between the touch and the healing of the woman, implying that the woman was healed immediately.
- The religious rulers got upset and confronted the crowd about Jesus's healing
- Jesus rebuked them and told them the Sabbath was made for man not the man for the Sabbath.
- Jesus then called the religious leaders hypocrites.
- He then asked them if they would have freed their animals from the stall if they needed water.
- Jesus is making note here that humans are more important to God than are animals.
- In other words, he is saying, if it feels right to lose an animal then it must be right to lose a daughter of Abraham.

The second thing that happened in this story is an argument broke out between Jesus, the religious leaders and the crowd that were in the synagogue. The goal of this study is to provide thoughtful insights, reflection of the principles and the importance of this text.

The religious leaders
- The rulers of the synagogue who witnessed Jesus healing on the Sabbath became indignant.
- This was not the first report of Jesus healing on the Sabbath.
- There is a similar story in Mark's Gospel where he healed a man with a withered hand and a man with dropsy.
- They were upset, but they did not address Jesus directly.
- They addressed the crowd.
- Instead of rebuking Jesus, they told everyone what Jesus had done in a negative way.

- They had probably heard about Jesus besting other religious leaders when they challenged him directly, so they spoke to the ground.
- They informed the crowd that they should not expect to be healed on the Sabbath.
- They directed them to come back on another day if they wanted to be healed.
- Their argument consisted of the fact that the woman had already been sick for 18 years and there seemed to be no danger of her dying.
- So, the religious rulers were suggesting that Jesus should honor God and keep the Sabbath holy by coming back on another day and healing her after the Sabbath had ended.
- This was probably also in order to keep anyone else from seeking healing on that date.
- They had probably heard about Jesus healing one person after another and they wanted to stop the train before it got started.

The multitude or crowd

- The multitude was disappointed because of the Pharisees address to them about the woman's healing.
- However, they rejoiced at the fact that Jesus healed her anyway.
- The Scripture says they glorified Jesus for the things that were done by him.
- This crowd was probably built of people who knew what it was like to have problems and to suffer, and who needed freedom from their illnesses.
- Because ordinary people are often attacked or criticized by those who have authority, they were happy to see the religious leaders receive rebuke from Jesus.
- They were probably happy to see that this religious leader had been put in his place because he had probably put them in their places many times.

Questions

The questions that follow are for the purpose of pointing out the Bible truths in the passage, God's authority, Salvation and much more.

- The Bible says Jesus saw the woman. The question was asked, what did he see when he saw the woman?
- The next question, Jesus called the woman over to him. By what name did he call her? -
- The next question, was the woman who had been bent for 18 years going to church for 18 years?
- The last thing is, he touched her. Where did he touch her, on the spot where she was bent, on the head or the hand or where?
- Why were the religious rulers upset?
- Why did the rulers tell the people to come back?
- Why did Jesus heal the woman?

In order to gain a hearing and to overcome the resistances one faces in gaining that hearing, the preacher must remain faithful to the calling of revealing what God has spoken in the Holy Bible. This what we have been called to do, to express God's glory in and beyond our cultural context.

Appendix Two – Sermon Notes

Sermon Number 1

"Praise God for His Wonderful Works"
Luke 13:12-14,17

When he said this, all his opponents were put to shame; and the entire crowd was rejoicing at all the wonderful things that he was doing. NRSV

I wonder, how many of you are grateful for the wonderful things God has done for you. Come on, don't play with me, are you really thankful? I am asking you that in the beginning because I don't think many of us really understand how grateful we ought to be for the wonderful things God has done.

I. Introduction

    A. Yet the Psalmist in #107 makes it clear that we ought to praise God. Look at it.

- In verse number 8, a powerful verse right here, David says, Oh, that *men* would praise the LORD *for* his goodness, and *for* his wonderful works to the children of men!
- Then, he writes another powerful verse, in verse 15 he says, Oh, that *men* would praise the LORD *for* his goodness, and *for* his wonderful works to the children of men!
- Then, he gets real deep and amplifies it in verse 21 and says, Oh, that *men* would praise the LORD *for* his goodness, and *for* his wonderful works to the children of men!
- Then, it just blows up because this is what he really wants you all to hear: he wraps it up in verse 31, Oh

that *men* would praise the LORD *for* his goodness, and *for* his wonderful works to the children of men!

B. Apparently, David thinks that the works of God are wonderful. So, every time David thinks about God, every time David writes about God, every time David reflects on God.

He just cries, Oh, that *men* would praise the LORD *for* his goodness, and *for* his wonderful works to the children of men!

In other words, the psalmist is like, dude, praise him. Don't sit there and look at me, praise him! Don't wait on someone else to praise him, you praise him. David says, Oh, that *men* would praise the LORD *for* his goodness, and *for* his wonderful works to the children of men!

The Hebrew word translated here as "wonderful":

☐ Denotes something indescribably great;
☐ That which is so tremendous and so amazing, it's literally beyond all description;
☐ It speaks of that which goes beyond human comprehension.

C. A Wonderful Miracle Worker

Tell your neighbor, He is a wonderful miracle worker. According to Luke, this miracle in our text, actually took place in one of the Synagogues. And, as was His custom, Jesus went into the synagogue to teach on the Sabbath and while He was there He performed a miracle.

D. Now, I believe one of the reasons this is such a wonderful story is because God allows us to see this miracle from several different perspectives.

We see it from the vantage point of:

- ☐ Mainly, the one it was done for
- ☐ But also, of the ones who witnessed it
- ☐ As well as the One who did it

II. Bowed for 18 Years

A. The bible says that amongst them which were there on that Sabbath Day was a woman who had been bowed over for the past 18 years. The scripture doesn't say it, but it is implied that for 18 years; although, she could not lift herself up, she was permitted and willfully went to public worship. Some of us because we think it is the church's job to straighten us up, would have quit or changed churches long before now. 18 years, we would have probably got tired of trying.

But, not this lady.

- ☐ 18 years, same thing nothing is changed.
- ☐ 18 years, same stops, same journey.
- ☐ 18 years, the same people.

However, because of her love and loyalty to God, she stayed
right there.

B. I'm just saying, although she was bound, she did not let what she was going through keep her from worshipping God. And, I believe it was her patience and persistence that led to this miracle.

- ☐ She was in church.
- ☐ She was bent.
- ☐ She could not straighten herself up.

C. But, she worshiped God anyway. Why, I don't know, I would imagine it is because she was a daughter of Abraham, and as a daughter of Abraham, although she was broken down at the time, she was still a woman with a promise. Yes, the bad news was she was broken down, stalled on her way to greatness, but the good news was she had a promise.

Look at someone and say broke down with a promise. Yes, and I wonder if there is a witness today that can say, been there done that, got the T-Shirt. I was on my way to greatness and had a breakdown on my way to my promise?

Anybody ever been:

- ☐ broke with a promise
- ☐ lonely with a promise
- ☐ left to yourself with a promise

III. On Your Way to Your Promise

A. I am just asking, is there anyone, other than me who has ever been stalled or bogged down on your way to your promise?

Sometimes, I feel like the story told about a large two-engine train that was crossing Canada. The story says after the train had gone some distance, one of the engines broke down. The engineer thought oh well, no problem, and carried on at half power.

But as the train got farther on down the line, the other engine broke down, and the train came to a standstill. So, the engineer decided he should inform the passengers about why the train had stopped, and so he made the following announcement:

He said: Ladies and gentlemen, I have some good news and some bad news. The bad news is that both engines have failed, and we will be stuck here for some time. The good news is that you decided to take the train and not fly.

Have you ever been there? Have you ever had everything around you dissipate, fall apart around you and then the one you were?

- ☐ hoping in,
- ☐ and trusting in,
- ☐ married to, engaged to

walks out on you, leaves you, and leaves you by yourself.

Have you ever been there?

- ☐ you already tired of struggling
- ☐ you already tired of trying to make it
- ☐ you already tired of trying to hold it together

and then, here comes something else! A pink slip.

I'm not talking about something in your dresser drawer or your closets ladies. I am talking about a pink slip from a job, somebody talking about we don't need you anymore. You been working for this company for years and is almost retirement time, but they got smart and said we are going to get rid of you before you reach retirement qualifications or retirement age.

And now, you are too old to labor or to work with your hands. And, you are not technological enough to have a good job in this current society. So, there you are stuck between Earth and glory.

- ☐ broke down

- ☐ with nothing
- ☐ with nobody
- ☐ with no way
- ☐ with no substance

stuck, bogged down on your way to your promise.

The promise is not fulfilled and everything around you that kept you so far is gone. Maybe you haven't been there, but I have. Yes, the bad news was, I was stuck between the break down and my promise. But the good news, I was closer than I thought.

B. I need you to help me help somebody. I want you to tell someone something and say it like you mean it. Tell someone, you are closer than you think. And, I need to drop a pen right here and tell somebody that when you get close to your promise the devil will fight you.

He will come and try to keep you

- ☐ from obeying
- ☐ from staying put
- ☐ from believing God.

That is why you have to graduate from the school of patience.

How do I know? Because there are tribulations in this land. And James says tribulations worketh patience; patience experience; experience hope; and hope make it not ashamed.

C. That is why, like this woman, we must learn how to

- ☐ Stay put
- ☐ Hold on, hang in there
- ☐ Don't go looking for another leader or for something else to follow

God's got this. Tell somebody, God's got this.

IV. Receiving Your Miracle

But, in order to get your miracle,

- ☐ you're going to have to learn patience
- ☐ you're going to have to demonstrate patience
- ☐ and you're going to have to deal with patience

In other words, tell somebody you're going to have to go through something. I am just saying, this woman was broken down with a promise and she had to go through a lot, but her persistence and her patience brought her to this time, to a place where Jesus could see her.

And I want to tell you that through your persistence and patience in seeking God, everything you have been through on your Christian journey has been for this time.

- ☐ Every setback you have experienced, it was for now
- ☐ Every time you were laid off, it was for now
- ☐ Every time somebody walked out on you, it was for now
- ☐ Every repo, every bankruptcy, it was for now
- ☐ Every struggle and fight you have ever had in your mind and with people in the kingdom or the world, it was for now
- ☐ Every time you have been misunderstood, talked about, lied on, it was for now

It was to get you to the place where Jesus can:

- ☐ see you, call you
- ☐ speak a word over your life
- ☐ and put his hands on you

Luke says, Jesus saw this woman. If somebody would ask me what he saw?

He looked at this woman and saw:

☐ She had proven she wasn't going anywhere
☐ She had proven that she realized whatever happens, God will take care of her
☐ She had proven that she had found God to be her reward and he's had her back
☐ Mama and daddy forsook, but the Lord took her in and now it was her time.

I am just saying, there comes a time when you must realize it is just you and God. And God's got this! Tell somebody, God's got this. Help is on the way!

And nobody else has to see what God is doing in your life as long as Jesus sees you and calls you! Because when he calls you, he calls you forward. Not backwards but forward.

Luke says, He calls her forward and speaks a word over her life saying woman you are free.

☐ You have been through the storm and the rain, but you made it
☐ you have been left alone, but it did not kill you
☐ you have been wounded but you can stand up
☐ you ended up in a hog pen, but you came to yourself and the father has received you.

And when He put his hands on her, the bible says immediately she stood up straight and praised God. I don't know what she said, but up above my head I hear music in the air and I imagine she said, He touched me. Oh, He touched me.

V. *God Has a Plan for You*

And some of you are praising God too because you are free from Satan's grip and there is nothing that can stop you now.

- ☐ This is the moment you've been waiting for.
- ☐ This is the acceptable time.
- ☐ This is your year of Jubilee.

You've been through too much to give up, and you're not going anywhere now. If there is anyone who can say?

- ☐ The devil should have killed you when he had you.
- ☐ He should have kept you when you were in his possession.

Because, now, Jesus has said you are free and you have wiggled yourself loose and you have remembered God has a plan for your life.

That is all I am saying. And that is the kind of people I want to lead. People, who it doesn't take all that pumping and priming

- ☐ You remember where you were when he found you.
- ☐ You remember where you were when he picked you up.
- ☐ And you remember where you were when he did it again.

You just remember the wonderful things God has done, and you praise Him.

VI. *Conclusion*

And that is exactly what happened in our text; Luke says after this miracle had taken place the synagogue leader was angry because Jesus healed on the Sabbath day. He said to the people, 'There are six days when one has to work. So, come to be healed on one of those days, and not on the Sabbath day." This seems like such a strange criticism. Why would someone get so angry over something as kindhearted and considerate as what Jesus did for this crippled woman? Not only that, but if people did come back on some other day—who was going to heal them?

Jesus was a busy man, traveling from one town to another. Who's to say he would even be there another day. This synagogue leader certainly didn't have the ability to perform miracles of healing the way Jesus did. But none of that seemed to matter to him.

He was:

- ☐ Blinded by his anger.
- ☐ Furious because Jesus had apparently broken the rules. But after Jesus set them straight, they were ashamed, and the entire crowd rejoiced at all the wonderful things that Jesus was doing.

What wonderful works? Let me help you. When I Look at this world that we are living in right now, filled with: Injustice, Wars and rumors of wars, Fires, tropical storms, tornadoes, floods, and hurricanes practically every week,

And I realize that in the midst of all this, we still have:

- ☐ Clothes on our backs,
- ☐ A roof over our head,
- ☐ And food on our table.

I want to Praise.

And when I look at our children, they may not be the smartest children in the classroom but at least they are healthy enough to go to school. As a matter of fact, there are some people who wish they had children, and if you have some you ought to thank God that you were able to have children.

You may not like your job but at least you have a job. What if you were unemployed, you really wouldn't like that. So, you need to give God praise. Somebody ought to say excuse me preacher, I owe God some praise right there because my job ain't really what it ought to be, but:

- ☐ I believe if I praise God right now in the middle of it
- ☐ I believe if I did not wait until I got the promotion
- ☐ I believe if I did not wait until the other company called me

I would just bless the Lord right now, I believe God.

And while I cannot speak for anyone else, although I might not really understand how much praise I owe God, when I think of the goodness of Jesus and all that he has done for me my soul cries hallelujah, and I give God some Praise because of what God has done.

And then again, when we think about what God is going to do because of his promise he has made, even if it is just heaven that is enough to shout about right there, because the Scripture says do not rejoice because the demons are subject to you, rejoice that your names have been written in heaven.

So, if your name:

- ☐ is on high
- ☐ and if heaven is your home
- ☐ and if you are going to live with God in glory
- ☐ if you are going to walk the streets of gold
- ☐ and if you are going to be there for his eternity

Then why do you have to wait to shout? You don't have to wait till you get there, you can practice right here because up there will be howdy, howdy and praise all day all long. I need someone who will give God a crazy praise right now for what He has already done. Come on give him a crazy praise, give him a crazy shout!

Sermon Number 2

"The Story behind My Praise"
Luke 13:12-14,17

I understand that for the past several weeks, you have been talking about the miracles of Jesus. Well the miracle we are looking for is are here,

On a Sabbath, Jesus was teaching in one of the synagogues, and a woman was there who had been crippled by a spirit for eighteen years. She was bent over and could not straighten up at all. When Jesus saw her, he called her forward and said to her, "Woman, you are set free from your infirmity." Then he put his hands on her, and immediately she straightened up and praised God. Indignant because Jesus had healed on the Sabbath, the synagogue leader said to the people, "There are six days for work. So, come and be healed on those days, not on the Sabbath." The Lord answered him, "You hypocrites! Doesn't each of you on the Sabbath untie your ox or donkey from the stall and lead it out to give it water? Then should not this woman, a daughter of Abraham, whom Satan has kept bound for eighteen long years, be set free on the Sabbath day from what bound her?" When he said this, all his opponents were humiliated, but the people were delighted with all the wonderful things he was doing. (Luke 13:10-17 NIV)

I. Introduction

According to Luke, this actually took place in one of the Synagogues that Jesus was teaching in on the Sabbath. Now, I believe one of the reasons this is such a wonderful story is because God allows us to see this miracle from several different perspectives.

We see it from the vantage point of:

- ☐ the one it was done for,
- ☐ the ones who witnessed it,
- ☐ and the One who did it,

II. Bowed for 18 Years

A. The bible says while Jesus was teaching, He saw a woman who had been crippled 18 years by a spirit that kept her so bent that she could not lift herself up. The NIV says, she could not straighten up at all.

B. And I believe it was her patience and persistence that led to this miracle

C. But she worshiped God anyway.

D. Broken down with a promise. Yes, the bad news was she was broken down, stalled on her way to greatness, but the good news was she had a promise.

III. On Your Way to Your Promise

    A. I am just asking, is there anyone who has ever been stalled or got bogged down on your way to your promise?

    B. The promise is not fulfilled and everything around you that kept you so far is gone.

    C. That is why you must graduate from the school of patience. How do I know, because there are tribulations in this land.

IV. Receiving Your Miracle

In other words, tell somebody you're going to have to go through something. I am just saying, this woman was broken down with a promise and she had to go through a lot, but her persistence and her patience brought her to this time, to a place where Jesus could see her.

And I want to tell you that through your persistence and patience in seeking God, everything you have been through on your Christian journey has been for this time. It was to get you to the place where Jesus could see you!

The Bible says Jesus

    ☐ saw her
    ☐ called her forward
    ☐ Spoke a word over her life saying you are set free from your infirmity.
    ☐ and put his hands on her

What did he see?

He looked at this woman and he saw that

- ☐ she had proven she wasn't going anywhere
- ☐ she had proven that she realized whatever be tide God will take care of her
- ☐ she had proven that she had found God to be her reward
  so, when he saw her, he called her forward and put his hands on her.

And, when He put his hands on her, immediately she stood up straight and praised God.

I don't know what she said, but I imagine she said: He touched me. Oh, He touched me.

V. *God Has a Plan for You*

That's the story behind her praise -- she remembered

- ☐ you remember where you were when he found you
- ☐ you remember where you were when he picked you up
- ☐ and you remember where you were when he did it again

Just remember the wonderful things God has done and you can praise him.

Sometimes, I sit, and I think of what God has done for me, where he has brought me from and I get happy.

[209]

VI. Conclusion

And that is the story behind my praise too! Every time I think of the goodness of God and the wonderful things He has done for me I give Him a praise!

When I look at this world we are living in right now, I realize in the midst of all this,

- we still have clothes on our back
- a roof over our head
- food on our table

I want to Praise.

And when I look at our children, they may not be the smartest children in the classroom, but at least they are healthy enough to go to school. As a matter of fact, there are some people who wish they had children, and if you have some you ought to thank God that you were able to have children.

You may not like your job but at least you have a job. What if you were unemployed, you really wouldn't like that. So, you need to give God praise. Somebody ought to say excuse me preacher, I owe God some praise right there because my job ain't really what it ought to be, but

- I believe if I praise God right now in the middle of it
- I believe if I did not wait until I got the promotion
- I believe if I did not wait until the other company called me

I would just bless the Lord right now.

Sermon Number 3

"Church on The Sabbath"
Luke 13:12-14,17

On a Sabbath Jesus was teaching in one of the synagogues, and a woman was there who had been crippled by a spirit for eighteen years. She was bent over and could not straighten up at all. When Jesus saw her, he called her forward and said to her, "Woman, you are set free from your infirmity." Then he put his hands on her, and immediately she straightened up and praised God. Indignant because Jesus had healed on the Sabbath, the synagogue leader said to the people, "There are six days for work. So, come and be healed on those days, not on the Sabbath." The Lord answered him, "You hypocrites! Doesn't each of you on the Sabbath untie your ox or donkey from the stall and lead it out to give it water? Then should not this woman, a daughter of Abraham, whom Satan has kept bound for eighteen long years, be set free on the Sabbath day from what bound her?" When he said this, all his opponents were humiliated, but the people were delighted with all the wonderful things he was doing. (Luke 13:10-17 NIV)

I. Introduction

According to Luke, in this parable, Jesus, on the Lord's Day was in the Lord's house. Ok. Let me say it another way.

- ☐ Jesus, the Divine
- ☐ Jesus, the incarnate one
- ☐ Jesus, the third person of the trinity

Was in the Lord's house on the Lord's Day

Okay, you still did not get it. I just said, Jesus

[211]

- ☐ Who was all that
- ☐ Who is all that
- ☐ And will be all that

Was in church on the Lord's Day.

Okay, one more time. Jesus went to the house that was ordained to bless His Daddy, on the day His Daddy had ordained to be blessed. Which says to me that we ought not ever act like it is alright to miss church, just because

- ☐ We have a golf game
- ☐ Or you have to wash your car
- ☐ Or you have company in from out of town
- ☐ Or stuff ain't going right

No. I think we need the Lord more than Jesus did and if Jesus went to church so should we.

Now, don't miss this. The bible says that Jesus was in the Lord's house on the Lord's Day, and what was he doing? He was teaching. Yes, that is right. Believe it or not Jesus use to teach in the church. Tell somebody he use to. He use to be invited to church to teach.

II. Bowed for 18 Years

A. Let me move on, the bible says that while Jesus was teaching He saw a woman who had been crippled 18 years by a spirit that kept her so bent that she could not lift herself up. The NIV says, she could not straighten up at all.

For 18 years this woman has lived like this.

- ☐ Where has she been for 18 years?
- ☐ What has she been doing for 18 years?
- ☐ What kept her going for 18 years?

I do not know. All I know is on this day she was permitted and was willfully in church worshiping God!

18 years, is a long time to be wrestling with an infirmity. Most people would have probably got tired of waiting and just gave up. But, not this woman! This woman who had this infirmity for 18 years was where on the Sabbath? She was in church.

☐ She was bent
☐ She could not straighten herself up

But she worshiped God anyway.

B. She was like the old woman who was dreadfully crippled with rheumatism that used to hobble to church on two canes. A friend asked her one day, Betty, how do you manage it? She looked at her friend and said, my heart gets there first and my old legs follow on after.

Likewise, this woman in our text obviously had a love for and loyalty to God that even in times like these, sustained her! I'm just saying, although she was bound she did not let what she was going through keep her from worshipping God.

Why, --I don't know. Maybe she understood what David meant when he said.

☐ Ps 122:1, I was glad when they said unto me, let us go into the house of the Lord!
☐ Ps 84:1, How lovely are thy tabernacles, O Lord of hosts.

Or, maybe it is because she knew, as a daughter of Abraham she was an heir to a promise. Who knows? I

[213]

mean look at the text. We do not even know who this woman was. All we know is Jesus was teaching in the synagogue and this woman was in the congregation.

We know she had not used her physical condition as an excuse for missing the service, despite her deformity and the trial of being gawked at by strangers. She had come to the place where the word of God was taught and where God's people met together.

- ☐ We know she did not forsake the assembly of those who sought God's blessing. And truly, her faithful attendance was rewarded.
- ☐ She came sorrowing but went home rejoicing.
- ☐ Came suffering but went home healed.
- ☐ Came with a burden but went home singing and rejoicing.

And we know that had she missed that service, she would have missed the blessing of Jesus. For we have no record that He ever went back to that synagogue again.

This woman had a promise of greatness that she had not yet received. So, while she may be broken down right now, she was still a woman with a promise. Yes, the bad news was she was broken down, stalled on her way to greatness, but the good news was she had a promise.

I wonder if there is a witness today other than me that can say, I was on my way to greatness and had a breakdown on my way to my promise?

Anybody ever been:

- ☐ broke with a promise
- ☐ lonely with a promise
- ☐ left to yourself with a promise

III. On Your Way to Your Promise

A. I am just asking, is there anyone other than me who has ever been stalled or bogged down on your way to your promise? Have you ever been there? Have you ever had everything around you dissipate fall apart around you and then the one you were?

☐ hoping in,
☐ trusting in,
☐ married to, engaged to,
   then walks out on you and leaves you by yourself.

Have you ever been there?

☐ you are already tired of struggling
☐ you are already tired of trying to make it
☐ you are already tired of trying to hold it together
   and then here comes something else!

IV.   *Receiving Your Miracle*

The Bible says when Jesus:

☐ saw her
☐ called her forward
☐ spoke a word over her life saying you are set free from your infirmity.
☐ and put his hands on her

What did he see?

He looked at this woman and he saw that:

☐ she had proven she wasn't going anywhere

- [ ] she had proven that she realized whatever she was tide of God will take care of her
- [ ] she had proven that she had found God to be her reward so, when he saw her, he called her forward and put his hands on her.

And when He put his hands on her, immediately she stood up straight and praised God. I don't know what she said, but I imagine she said: He touched me. Oh, He touched me.

VI. Conclusion -Why do many lack the zeal of this good woman in coming to the House of God?

Once God is enthroned in the heart, these fancied difficulties vanish away. Our feelings about the Lord's Day, shows the state of our souls. Will a man rob God of His glory, of His worship?

A Chinese preacher speaking of robbing God used this illustration. It came to pass that a man went to market with a string of seven coins. Seeing a beggar who asked for alms, he gave him 6 coins and kept one for himself. The beggar, instead of being thankful, followed the good man and stole the seventh coin also.

What a detestable wretch. Yes, God has given us six days. Are we stealing the other day also? If we cannot enjoy a few hours together each week in God's worship, it is very plain that we cannot enjoy an eternity in His presence in the world to come.

He is the same yesterday, today, and forever. Let us hold fast this blessed truth and never let it go. Our sins may be many, our lives worthless, but if we have the least desire for forgiveness and will come to Him in the spirit of repentance, there is hope for us. He can cleanse us from every sin and untie us from our infirmity. And, He will do it, not because we are worthy but because He loves us and knows that we cannot do it ourselves.

As D.H. Moody once said, "Men will never find salvation until they give up all efforts to save themselves." Someone asked an Indian how he had gotten converted. Before he said anything, he built a fire in a circle and placed a worm within the circle. And then after the worm had crawled around every way for escape and had lain down to die, the Indian reached over and took him out. Then he said, "I was the worm in the circle. The fire of God's wrath was closing in on me. There was no escape. I gave up my struggles and the Lord Jesus went through the fire and saved me." We are not saved by our good works.

We are saved by the grace and love, and mercy of our Lord Jesus Christ who died on the cross for our sins. He will forgive us and untie us from our sins if we look to Him. He says, "Look unto me and be ye saved all the ends of the earth, for I am God and there is none else."

"I know that thou canst do everything. For prayer changes things, it changes men, however deep in sin. It brings them to the feet of the one who died for their hearts to win. Prayer changes things, for you and me, whatever be the case. Just bring it to the throne of grace and wait for the answered prayer." All things are possible to him that believeth.

We are saved by the grace and love, and mercy of our Lord Jesus Christ, who died on the cross for our sins.

Appendix Three – Evaluations

Evaluation Letter

Hello my friends,

As you may or may not be aware, I am in school, working on my Doctor of Ministry degree. I have made it to the final stage which is my project assignment. The topic of my project is _Black, Female and a Preacher: Sermonic Strategies for Overcoming Resistance to Gaining a Hearing in and Beyond Her Cultural Settings._ The purpose of this project is to identify, form and field-test some specific sermonic strategies to equip a black female preacher to face and overcome resistance to her challenging message, both in and beyond her cultural setting. One of the things I must do in this project is to receive feedback from sermons I will preach in a multicultural, a Hispanic, and a Caucasian congregation. Thus, I am asking in advance for your participation in completing an extensive sermon evaluation on the message you hear me preach. The evaluation will be emailed to you if you agree to accept the challenge to help me with my project. After carefully filling in all information, I would appreciate your emailing the evaluation back to me within a week from the time you hear the sermon. If you would like to participate, please respond to this email with a yes and I will forward you the evaluation.

Thank you for your help.

Ella McDonald

Evaluation Form

Rev. Ella M. McDonald
Sermon Evaluation Form

Name of Evaluator:

The Sermon Text:

Evaluator Culture:

Age of Evaluator: 20-40 ___; 41-60___; 61-80___; over 80___

I. The Biblical Text:

> A. Was the sermon's theological claim faithful to selected text?
>
> B. Did the text really make a difference for this sermon?

II. The Congregational Context:

> A. Did the sermon's choice of themes, imagery, stories, etc. reflect a respect for your cultural context?
>
> B. Did the sermon connect to some place of importance in your cultural context?

III. The Claim of the Sermon:

> A. Sermonic Focus: Was the sermon organized around a controlling thought, main theme, or idea? If so, in a complete sentence, state the sermon's focus as you experienced it.
>
> B. Sermonic Function: What do you think the sermonic aim was? Did it call you, the hearer to some sort of action or change, etc.?

IV. Sermonic Form: Did the sermon unfold in a consistent manner that you could follow with your listening ear? If so,

A. Was there a logical progression of thought that enabled you to follow without getting lost?

B. Were transitions smooth or disconnected?

V.   Illustrative Material- Were the illustrations practical in relation to contemporary life situations? If so,

A. What stories were helpful? Why?

B. Which were not? Why?

VI.   Constructive Feedback: Please respond to the following items concerning my delivery and presence: Evaluate each using this scale as a guide: 1–excellent; 2–good; 3–average; 4–poor; 5–unsatisfactory.

A. Delivery -*Please add comments beside each if you desire.*

___a. Volume

___b. Use of gestures

___c. Rate of speech

___d. Articulation

___e. Eye contact

___f. Use of notes/manuscript

B. Presence - -*Please add comments beside each if you desire.*

___a. Did my attire seem appropriate to you?

___b. Was there anything distracting about it?

___c. What was your view of my posture while sitting or standing?

___d. While preaching did I portray an attitude of self-importance or humility?

VII.   What did you find especially helpful about this sermon?

VIII.   What could have made this a better sermon?

IX.   If you could choose three adjectives to describe how I came across while preaching, what would they be?

X.   According to your understanding of the preaching of the Gospel of Jesus Christ and its benefits, did my personal flare and originality challenge, comfort, and encourage you to hear the word of God? If so how? If not, why?

Best Written Responses from Each Church

Written Response to (1A):

> From AME Church, Garland - Yes, you explained the text from 3 perspectives: the person being healed; the person healing; and the witnesses.

> From UMC Mabank – Yes, the faith of the woman and the practice of Jesus healing; God's relationship to the world shows that it does not matter what day Jesus heals, every day is God's day. We were told the story of a woman who was suffering until she met Jesus. It encouraged us to also believe Jesus will heal us in any way we need it.

From UMC Mesquite – No one gave a written explanation.

Written Response to (1B):

From AME Church, Garland - Yes! This sermon was so full of hope. It had characteristics of everyday life and existence. People can relate to taking care of animals every single day, not leaving them un-watered just because it is the Sabbath – to do that would be cruel, unkind.

From UMC Mabank -Yes, very much so. You related the miracle of Jesus healing the woman who had been crippled for 18 years in comparison to our congregation. Her undivided love for God kept her going and should keep us going.

From UMC Mesquite - Definitely, it was the basis of the sermon.

Question Number Two - The Congregational Context had two questions: Did the sermon's choice of themes, imagery, stories, reflect a respect for your cultural context? Did the sermon connect to some place of importance in your cultural context? All respondents from all three churches answered yes to both questions (100%).

Written Response to (2A):

From AME Church, Garland - The majority of the congregation of the church that I attended was black. Listening to the sermon and the imagery or examples that were presented by the Pastor were, in my opinion, were addressed to the black members. However, I felt that even though there was a diverse group of cultures/backgrounds in attendance at the sermon, the sermon's focus or message and usage of imagery were able to cross over any culture barriers.

From UMC Mabank – Extremely relatable in my culture of work & friends - Jesus can see and knows my breakdowns - just like the 18 years the woman struggled in the text. I didn't sense any disrespect for my culture at all but felt that Ella brought relatable issues as examples of breakdowns we might experience.

From UMC Mesquite - Yes, you gave examples of what you thought the individuals in the text may have felt thought or physically gone through. Then you related it back to how we may feel the same and put in your own personal story.

Written Response to (2B):

From AME Church, Garland - Yes, the text really did make a difference for this sermon because it was the foundation of the message. Throughout, we were told, "God's got this," "You're going to have to go through something," "you've been through too much to stop now," "remember where you were when God found you," etc. They all related right back to the Scripture.

From UMC Mabank – Many of my friends have struggled with making the mortgage payment. In fact, we sold our house to downsize so that we could make our payments without as much struggle. So, I felt that within my culture, we could identify with the illustrations and the theme. The part about being thankful and happy even when things are not going your way was relatable as well. An example Ella mentioned of some people not being able to have children was very identifiable. It reminded me to be thankful in ALL things. There is too much grumbling in my world...

From UMC Mesquite - Yes, that the Jesus has recused me from Satan. He has unbound me from my infirmity. Whether physical or emotional, he has released me.

Question Number Three - The Claim of the Sermon had two questions:

Sermonic Focus: Was the sermon organized around a controlling thought, main theme, or idea? If so, in a complete sentence, state the sermon's focus as you experienced it. Sermonic Function: What do you think the sermonic aim was? Did it call you, the hearer to some sort of action or change, etc.? All respondents from all three churches answered yes to both questions (100%).

Written Response to (3A):

> From AME Church, Garland - Yes, there was a central theme; and, there were several "sub-themes" that blended well with the sermon and re-enforced key points.

> From UMC Mabank – Yes! Hope! If so, in a complete sentence, state the sermon's focus – as I experienced it – hope and patience are tools from god to be used to bring me closer to him. I am a daughter of Abraham too; just like the woman in the story. We all have a promise of hope that allows us to keep going; we all have bad news or a stumbling block that hinders us, but she had that

promise of hope, and that god called her to church; we are all still on our way to him, and sometimes we might be 'broke down with a promise,' but we still can seek him.

From UMC Mesquite - Praise God in the midst of your situation; patience and persistence can lead to a miracle. We were given the example of the woman who had attended synagogue for 18 years despite her crippling illness, and her patience was rewarded.

Written Response to (3B):

From AME Church, Garland - From my perspective I believe the sermonic aim was to never lose focus of the compassion and love Jesus has for people. His love should always be the center of all we do as leaders. In addition, I won't allow religious legalistic perspectives deter me from seeing God for myself. I was encouraged to complete the work God is giving me even though some people may not understand it or disagree with it because the final outcome is to be focused on God and pleasing Him. Give God praise NOW! Don't give up!

From UMC Mabank – Yes! When the Pastor cited

[227]

examples of "brokenness", I was able to say; "I've been there" too! Among the many thoughts that I took away from the sermon was to never give up. There is always someone who has it much worse and as long as you can sing praise to God, you are getting ready to worship God forever!

From UMC Mesquite - I think the sermon's aim was to give those who needed an uplifting this morning, those who were maybe feeling down, a boost to remember that our relationship with God is one that you need to renew each day, not letting excuses get in the way.

Question Number Four - Sermonic Form: Did the sermon unfold in a consistent manner that you could follow with your listening ear? Was there a logical progression of thought that enabled you to follow without getting lost? Were transitions smooth or disconnected? All respondents answered yes to all questions 100%.

Written Response to (4A) – Logical:

From AME Church, Garland - Yes, the scripture about the bent-over woman healed by Jesus was the thread that was used to connect the entire sermon.

From UMC Mabank – I never got lost. Rev. Ella stayed on track, keep praising God, keep your eyes on him. We've got the promise. Examples: when you have been deserted; you're by yourself. She asked the congregation 'been there?' Yes! Tired of struggling? Yes. To make it every day, to hold it together – then here comes something else – another stumbling block – a pink slip – you've been there for years and they don't need you anymore. You're laid off. You're stuck between earth and glory – but you've got the promise – this was repeated, over and over; you've got the promise.

From UMC Mesquite - Like the woman who was "bound," we all have stuff in our lives that keeps us from being all God/Jesus creates us to be -- I need to let Jesus touch me, and not give up!

Written Response (4B) - Flow:

From AME Church, Garland - Yes, I had no problems with the flow; however, I attend a church with a somewhat different method of presentation of the sermon. I thoroughly enjoyed the different way (for me) that the sermon was presented. Even found myself thinking how wonderful the raw emotion was and refreshing.

From UMC Mabank – Yes! You followed your introductory explanation of the bible verse and you used humor and personal stories to keep me involved, interested and during transitions.

From UMC Mesquite – No one wrote a response

Written Response (4C) – Transition:

From AME Church, Garland - The transitions were smooth and easy to not only follow; but easy to understand. During the sermon, I noted the varying ages of the congregation. It came to my attention that there were several young children. What impressed upon my mind was the attention that these young children (approximately 8-12 years of age) gave the Pastor.

From UMC Mabank – No response

From UMC Mesquite – No Response

Question Number Five - Illustrative Material: Were the illustrations practical in relation to contemporary life situations? If so, what stories were helpful? Which were not? Why? All respondents answered yes to all questions 100%.

Written Response (5A):

From AME Church, Garland - In my opinion, personal experience and testimonies within a sermon brings the text to life. The stories used allow people to see the reality of God working in the lives of people today. Since God is always in the moment, we as people need to see that as illustrated through the stories and personal testimonies you shared.

From UMC Mabank – The story about the train – the train had two engines; one broke down, then the other broke down; so, both engines are out; but the good news? You took the train instead of flying. Love that story, have used it since. And the illustration of losing a job – the not feeling needed or wanted anymore; I think everyone can relate to that.

From UMC Mesquite – The conversion story. In a circle of confusion with no way out until Jesus comes and lift you. Powerful! To get across the water, I have to get IN the water… Ever been broke down on the way to my promise? (Train engines story) I'm still alive and can still make it if I let Jesus take my hand and lead me. Where there's life, there's hope! It may look bad, but you are closer to God's promise than you think! When God calls, he (or she!☺) pulls you forward, not pushes you away! SO many of your phrases & questions and illustrations were very VISUAL (brought a picture to mind) and EVOCATIVE (brought a strong feeling to the surface)

Written Response (5B):

From AME Church, Garland – All were good.

From UMC Mabank – NA

From UMC Mesquite – No response

Question Number Six - Constructive Feedback: Please respond to the following items concerning my delivery and presence: Evaluate each using this scale as a guide: 1–excellent; 2–good; 3–average; 4–poor; 5–unsatisfactory. All categories except Delivery (c) and (d) were 100% ones. Two people (6%) said there were times when I got excited and they could not understand what I was saying. There were two people (6%) that said there were times when the intensity of my voice combined with the volume of the microphones was a little loud for them.

From AME Church, Garland - Constructive feedback: The delivery: Volume – your volume was fine but hold the drums back a bit, so I can hear you. Use of gestures – good; Rate of speech – when you get excited, you talk faster and it's harder to understand you Articulation – good; Eye contact – good – you looked all around, and back at the choir; now whether you were looking directly at me it was hard to tell because you had your glasses on, but you were not looking down, reading the sermon, which leads into the next: Use of notes, manuscript – if you had any I couldn't tell; you seemed to be preaching directly from the heart – and I have been in church when the sermon was read like a book from a script; you were totally opposite – it was as if you were preaching completely extemporaneously. Flowed so smooth and completely. Hope and patience and promise. Just kept flowing.

From UMC Mabank - Volume: Always just right. Use of gestures: You use your hands well. Rate of speech: Always just the right tempo—never too fast or slow. Articulation: Never a problem understanding you. Eye contact: You look to all parts of the sanctuary when you speak. Use of notes/manuscript: Not noticeable. Presence: Yes, black robe with red stole looked very nice. Was there anything distracting about it? Not at all. What was your view of my posture while sitting or standing? Tall and straight. While preaching did I portray an attitude of self-importance or humility? Humility, but not to the point of being ineffective; you also had great authority in your preaching.

From UMC Mesquite - Delivery Volume: There were 3 times that I missed a point that you made or end of a phrase that was kind of "thrown away" (volume, rate of speech and articulation), Use of gestures: Animated but not distracting Rate of speech (see a.) Articulation (see a.) Eye contact - and SMILE! Felt like you were talking right to ME! Use of notes/manuscript - knew it well enough to preach with little reference to notes; occasional "look" was done smoothly. Loved it when you closed the notebook toward the end and preached the rest of the way "untethered!" Presence - Did my attire seem appropriate to you? SO happy for you about your weight loss achievement! You look 10 years younger and healthier! ☺. Was there anything distracting about it? NO. What was your view of my posture while sitting or standing? Both "natural Ella" While preaching did I portray an attitude of self-importance or humility? Humility, and total openness to the Holy Spirit's leadings.

Question Number Seven - What did you find especially helpful about this sermon?

From AME Church, Garland - The promise of hope. Promises – I may think I'm stuck, but I'm closer than I think. God always has somebody, he always shows up. Watch out for Satan, he sends an imitator, a distraction – he tries to keep you from believing in god; but have patience and hope and keep showing up, just like the woman in the scripture, she showed up for 18 years with a crooked back that Jesus tells us was caused by demons. But she kept on showing up. She had hope. I liked the phrase, learn how to graduate from the school of patience; you just cannot have too much patience, you keep building on to your storeroom of hope. Through the promise. The promise that has come down from Abraham – the woman is specifically called a daughter of Abraham. He was called by God to leave his home, take his family and go; but he had faith, and believed in the promise of God. He didn't go

[235]

looking for something else to follow, he followed God. He knew God had a miracle for him, he had patience, and he demonstrated it. We all have to deal with troubles; we all have to go through something. But with persistence, patience and perseverance, seeking God, like the woman going to church every week for eighteen years, she had patience. And she met God; he spoke, laid hands on her, and healed her. It was her miracle. This gives us hope. She had been afflicted with demons, but she got to where Jesus saw her, had mercy and she was loosed from her bonds of suffering. What a powerful sermon, especially for a black church to hear, as the black race has been bound by bonds of suffering and slavery for centuries. It was a sermon of hope and promise.

From UMC Mabank – Personal illustrations shared about times when you struggled to meet the mortgage, or didn't have a car, etc. Showed a "realness" about Ella, that she KNOWS what it's like to be without and that she can relate to others. Taking the time to stop and sing "He Touched Me." Besides it is fitting right in with the text, it was very moving. I will never again hear that song without it meaning more to me. I can picture Jesus touching me and healing me. The promise that God will heal me and get me to where I'm going is powerful and this song helped with the concept. It gave a moment of reprieve to digest what all had been said and to ponder the words of a very familiar song.

From UMC Mesquite - The song, "He Touched Me" (One of my life favorites!! I cried as you sang!) "If you hadn't been through that, I wouldn't have needed to touch you! ...And He *keeps on* doing it! When Jesus is in the house -- healing, joy and love are there!

Question Number Eight - What could have made this a better sermon?

From AME Church, Garland - While I wish to be objective and provide constructive input on the sermon, I cannot in all honesty think of anything that would have made this a better sermon. Maybe more A/C...LOL!!!

From UMC Mabank – I especially connected with the message that sometimes we have to go through a lot of "stuff" or trials to strengthen our relationship with Jesus. There have been times in my life when I have been "broke down" and I know I cannot make it on my own without God!

From UMC Mesquite - Your explanation of the bible scripture and the way you broke down the parts, so I could relate to it and use it in my daily walk

Question Number Nine – If you could choose three adjectives to describe how I came across while preaching, what would they be?

From AME Church, Garland - Passionate. It was deeply passionate and loving towards the congregation. It was knowledgeable about the scripture, and the bible, it showed. And the last word would be humble. You are gifted to be able to preach god's word, not everyone can, and your thankfulness to god for this gift shows.

From UMC Mabank – Knowledgeable, Hopeful, Relatable.

From UMC Mesquite - (1) Compassionate, (2) Confident, and (3) Enthusiastic.

Question Number Ten - According to your understanding of the preaching of the Gospel of Jesus Christ and its benefits, did my personal flare and originality challenge, comfort, and encourage you to hear the word of God? If so how? If not, why?

From AME Church, Garland - Again, as stated earlier, my goal is to be as objective as possible and provide undiluted feedback. However, the Pastor's enthusiastic and heartfelt deliverance of the sermon was so uplifting and inspiring! I attend a fairly conservative church and have never attended a black church before. Although I had heard (and seen in movies) that the black people worship with such enthusiasm and volume, I sat spellbound not only by the Pastor's delivery of the sermon (which I must in all honesty admit distracted me from my note taking), but also by the reaction from the congregation. I was continually looking around at the faces and I felt so very much connected with them. I was amazed at one person in front of me who kept standing up and saying, "Thank You Jesus". I found myself thinking...I want that!

I had told my Sunday School group that I would miss that Sunday in order to attend this African Methodist Episcopal Church. When I arrived at my Sunday School class the following Sunday, the first thing I was asked was "how was it"? Here are my two comments: (1) I cannot ever remember being in such a spirit filled church. I could feel God's presence and His enjoyment of His people the entire time I was there; and (2) when I get to Heaven, I want to rejoice and worship God with the members of that congregation. It was so awesome!!

In closing, there are a couple of personal observations that I would like to make. First, I was impressed with the leadership and concern the Pastor demonstrated prior to the service. There was an extremely large turnout for the service. In fact, as more and more people arrived, the deacons had to continually bring out more chairs. It got to a point where the chairs had to be lined up against all of the walls and the aisle. I had to smile when I heard the Pastor request that some of the members move to the choir loft so that the visitors would have a place to sit. What an awesome problem to have!! I carefully observed the way that the Pastor handled not only the overflow and lack of chairs, but the fact that the air conditioner could not handle the capacity. I watched her discretely request the ushers to bring in more fans. Again, what a wonderful problem to be faced with! Also, during the sermon, the Pastor burst into the song "He Touched Me". I sat totally awestruck at the beauty and connection of that song to her message. I actually got goose bumps! After the service, a member of another church said to me...."we need more Preachers like her"! AMEN!!!

From UMC Mabank – Absolutely. You bring the stories from the Scriptures to life and make them so interesting and relevant! The energy with which you deliver the message is contagious and obviously comes straight from the Holy Spirit. Your message made me want to go out and be a better Christian!

Comparing the Two Contexts: I think if possible the Mabank sermon was even better than the Garland one. Maybe it was because I listened to it on the internet and wasn't distracted by people around me, but it seemed you had also polished the sermon to shine even brighter the following week. As you know, I've seen you preach many times, Ella, in both predominantly black and "mixed" contexts, but I always feel like it's the same Ella. Although you are sensitive to the congregations' differences and with a more predominantly white

[241]

congregation you may be a bit more reserved, you still bring enough of your fire and enthusiasm to the group that you enliven the place. There is never a moment of boredom.

The main difference I notice is that at your home church you have the musician backing you up, and that adds a certain drama. You also go into more elongated and passionate "runs," or whatever you call them, when you have a series of thoughts you string together to drive the point home at the end. Obviously the A.M.E. congregation is more comfortable with audience participation, but I love it when you challenge the more white audiences to express their feelings. I imagine that encourages you to feel more comfortable yourself in delivering the message—yet I also think that maybe not having that same affirmation from the mixed congregation hones your preaching skills even more.

Another difference I've noticed you rarely mention time in your home church, but you do mention it when you're preaching in a mixed context and I'm sure it's probably constraining for you (although it doesn't hurt your message at all)! There is more emotion from the pulpit in the A.M.E. context, and to be honest for someone coming from a very reserved white church sometimes this can be a little scary. I guess maybe there's a fear of the unknown since it's so different. Having been raised in a predominantly white church, * I'm more comfortable in the "mixed" context, but attending A.M.E. worship has stretched me, and, in many ways, I see how it is more liberating than the more "uptight" mixed contexts. (I selfishly would love to see you bring your gifts to dying UMC congregations. But at the same time, I know your heart is in A.M.E.)

From UMC Mesquite - Yes, because you chose a text where Jesus is active through His talk and His ministry. Jesus is the model I should follow and scriptures that reflect Him directly will always challenge me when I'm not doing what I'm supposed to, it will comfort me when I beat myself up for not being where I think I should be and it encourages me to let me know that I'm on the right track. Overall, your personality and originality made it easy to follow and easy to hear.

Unity Service Evaluations

A.   Feb 3 at 3:00 PM

Dear Pastor Ella,

Sorry I'm just now able to get back to you, but here's my input. I hope it can help you.

Organization: I thought that all was well organized. Since you deal with real people, something can always go wrong and if that happened that Sunday, we didn't know it. I thought that the program was easy to read and orderly. I like that each person's title and position was included. No questions to ask about any of the speakers. The visual "bullets" were clear and understandable. Very helpful.

Audience reaction: Everyone seemed very attentive to the whole program. We expected what was going to happen in the program except for when you asked us all to move next to someone we didn't know. As it can be in a normal gathering of people, most folks "group" together with those they know. Since the main theme of this day was "Unity in Diversity", I thought it was great when you asked everyone to switch seats. It definitely "broke the ice" and brought a coziness and familiarity to the crowd. It was unexpected but totally welcomed by the crowd.

Responses you heard: I heard everyone say how great that was. Everyone seemed to be receptive to meeting and sharing "love" for each other as worshipers of the same God. We may all worship differently but we all worship the same God. That gives us unity with each other. We are all brothers and sisters.

Response to the Bishop's preaching style, etc.: I totally enjoyed the Bishop in every way. I had seen her before the program, in the Ladies' room, and thought to myself, what a nice, pretty lady. She was getting dressed and I was washing my hands and we talked a little. What a joy for me to see her walk in with the other pastors and to see that she was the Bishop for the AME church. Being raised in an AME church, and now I attend United Methodist, I was very glad to see and acknowledge that we all have so much more in common, than different, in our church services. I was very proud of her intelligence and her spiritual connection to God. It was obvious as to how much she loves the Lord. She is a wonderful example for all women---especially for little black girls, to imagine what they can become when God uses them. I enjoyed her message and got a lot out of what she said. It was interesting to hear of her life and the common things we have to pray for. A blessing for me, and as I was told from those sitting around me, a blessing and joy for them.

Ella, I hope my "2 cents" helps you. Please let me know if I can do anything else. Of course, I will pray for you and all that you are trying to achieve. God be with you!

Love you,
Carlene Knuble

B.   My Observation:

In 2011, Rev. McDonald was given the charge to pastor the AME Church, in Garland, TX. It started out as a predominantly black congregation, but in almost three years of pastoring this church, the diversity of the membership has changed vividly! We now have two white males. One, a young man who is our base guitarist, and the other, an older gentleman that assists in the audio ministry sometimes. Going even further, we have received into full membership three Hispanic families, which in number is about fifteen people, including three or four adults and their children, ranging in age sixteen to two years old.

Although, everyone is aware of the diversity within the church, no one feels offended or divided. It's just the opposite, in that everyone is pretty much treated like family. The kids not only worship together, participate in the Young People's Department, but they play together. When altar prayer is done, our Hispanic members does not stand alone, but they stand with their sister's and brother's in Christ! When one member cries or goes to the altar for prayer, there are usually other members standing with them, in support or to console that person.

Like all the members who have attended the AME church for a short time or for many years, our white and Hispanic members take their walk with Christ, and their membership very seriously. They interact with the congregation as a whole. Each of them have their own personal relationship with Rev. McDonald. They support the church in their tithes and offering, as well as in their time. I believe this is due in part to Pastor McDonald's teaching. Her sincere love and devotion to God, His vision(s) and His people are displayed not only in the pulpit, but when interacting individually with each one of her members.

When giving their testimonies, some of the newest members, and most of the Hispanic population, will attest that they have never been a part of a church, and perhaps some never even step foot in a church, before joining this church. Nevertheless, since becoming a member, you can see their eagerness to know more about what it truly means to be a Christian, what it truly means to serve God, what it truly means to be loved unconditional by God, by their pastor and by the people they share membership with. This diverse congregation has come a long way to become a unified body of Christ, to be part of the connectional church, and not just our local church.

This diverse group of people are very intentional about being in church on Sunday's; they are excited about the worship experience, hearing the choirs sing, participating in Youth Sunday, and listening to Pastor McDonald preach the gospel in such a way that everyone, from the youngest to the oldest, can understand. Not only are the adults excited, but the young people are as well! Often times, it is the young members who bring their family and friends to church with them.

C. On January 26, 2014, The Church celebrated our Church Anniversary. Our theme was: *"Unity in Diversity: Christians Celebrating Doing What is Right and Good as Christ Would"!* Together with Rev. Dr. Joe Pool of Rockwall First United Methodist Church and Pastor McDonald organized a multi-cultural service, held at Rockwall FUMC. The main purpose was to join our church's predominantly black congregation with that of FUMC predominantly white congregation, in order to see if this could be done and how effective it would be. Not only were these two congregations joined together, but clergy and lay from all races, and other churches and denominations were assembled to witness this awe-inspiring day, and what a day it was! From entering the front doors of this very large, very beautiful edifice, we were met by Greeters who had smiles galore, offering to help wherever there was a need! Once everyone started to gather in the sanctuary, you could see the smiles on people's faces; black, white, and Hispanic alike. No one knew what to expect, but everyone waited in anticipation, not quite knowing what to expect! You could see the excitement in the room, as people joined with their congregations, their families and friends, to take part in this uncommon multicultural setting. Some looked anxious, but there were some who looked right at home.

Rev. McDonald enlisted a very close friend, who happens to be a member of the United Methodist Church, and from the Emmaus community, to oversee the praise part of the service. Now, you could perceive that some people were not totally in sync with a few of the song choices; however, since the entire program was on the big screens for everyone to see and follow, it made it easier to keep up. And, because of Rev. McDonald's person of choice to do this, she kept the congregation engaged in her humor! She had everyone singing a few songs that were out of the norm for some of the worshippers. But, overall, I could see that people were really engaged.

Now, Rev. McDonald did something that perhaps made a lot of people wish they had stayed home. In her opening, she expressed how good everyone looked, and how thankful she was that so many was in the house. But, she went a step further! She made the statement: "what would really look nice, is if everyone who is sitting with someone they already know, would please switch it up, and go sit with someone you don't know". Needless to say, some people were somewhat reluctant, but most respected her request and complied. Once the ice had been broken, I believe everyone felt a sense of ease. The repositioning and the service seemed to have flowed wonderfully! People were hugging and laughing.

Also, with the program participants being diverse, everyone in the congregation could relate, because they could see someone who looked just like them on the podium. I thought that was a brilliant idea! As every participant played a critical part in the program and how it flowed, I believe, because Rev. McDonald strategically placed everyone, that each person was indeed in their "right" place. It made the service flow better, it caused the worshippers to be more connected spiritually, it caused the worshippers to become more involved in the service, and it gave everyone a clearer understanding that this was going to be something much bigger than one could have ever imagined. From the Processional, the technical guy that kept the Power Point running smoothly, the Call to Worship, the musical selections, the powerful Litany, the liturgical dancers and the very on time sermon *"Building*

Bridges", you could see people standing to their feet, clapping in amazement, crying tears of joy, and even interacting with one another, to the point of giving each other high-fives!! It was spectacular to see so many, from different races, backgrounds and denominations, praise and worship God, in such a way that was almost too real to believe. Not that I witnessed any unwelcomed differences, and if there were any, people set them aside for such a time, and shared in an overwhelming, powerful display of adoration, appreciation and respect for God, and their sister's and brother's worshipping God on one accord!

Can this type of multi-cultural worship experience work and be effective? In my observation and honest opinion, I would say that on January 26, 2014, it undeniably worked.

D. An African Methodist Episcopal Church
Rev. Ella M. McDonald, Pastor
Church Anniversary Service – Sunday, January 26, 2014

Theme: Unity in Diversity: Doing What is Right and Good as Christ Would.

3 p.m. worship setting took place at First United Methodist Church in Rockwall, Texas. It was decided to have our evening service at this edifice not only because of the size of the sanctuary, but also because this congregation is mainly of White ethnicity, to which many of St. Luke members have not experienced before.

Bringing the two congregations together was a success – in worship and in unity. In my opinion and observation, having the two United Methodist's Churches come together at First United Methodist created a diverse setting that our church members did not know they could adapt to. Normally, when we have church anniversaries, our church invites other churches to come to worship with us. This setting took the church away from home and into an environment that was different for many.

My observation was that at the start of worship many within the congregation still chose to sit with people they already knew – feeling comfortable sitting near people that they normally fellowship with. A few did choose to sit with other denomination.

During the early part of worship, Pastor McDonald asked everyone to move to other seats and to mix and mingle with someone there that we did not know, and to greet and meet others there that we did not know already. You could see the diversity within this setting. People greeted one another with hugs, words of kindness, and excitement! Most everyone then sat next to people they did not know – of different race and/or culture. For a brief moment this felt a bit awkward to me, but that didn't last long. As I introduced myself to those now sitting on same pew, I began to realize that although some were African American just as I am, the others who were Anglo American were not much different.

Up and down the pew where I sat I could see and hear open communication now taking place as we got to know one another. I observed some extra greeting and hugs now taking place as we shared smiles, hugs, and the opportunity to be in this diverse setting! The awkwardness did not linger.

Not only was the congregation now diverse in culture, the chosen program participants included were of various cultures and backgrounds as well. Program participants included educational background, theological backgrounds, young students with vocal talents, young students with dance talents, and mix of Methodist and African Methodist denominations, diverse cultures!

However, although of visual diversity within this congregation – the result was Unity! The songs by the worship leader and choir were inspiring to the theme of this worship. The printed program included Liturgies and Scriptures relative to the theme of being unified while in a diverse setting. The preached word was delivered by a very prestigious Bishop, a woman of education and experience in ministry. Words of courage, dignity, power, motivation, forgiveness, love, hope – all created a powerful word for the people. There was laughter shared among us, friendships shared among us, questions and answers shared among us, and more so – unity within this setting.

Pastor McDonald's creative way of bringing the old – or former Pastor, back with the congregation he once Pastored; and Pastor McDonald's way of bringing the African American church to the Anglo church, in my observation and opinion created a diverse setting of old and new, black and white – created a sense of opposites joining together and creating a positive worship setting!

Dianna Thompson

E. Nancy

Organization: From the beautiful PowerPoint slides, to the impressive processional, to the amazingly smooth flow of the service, to the caliber of presenters and speakers, the high level of effort that went into organizing this event was evident.

Highlights:

- The clergy processional was impactful. It seemed to elevate the import of the occasion by the pageantry and ceremonial protocols that were followed, and it set the stage (literally!) for the magnitude of the occasion.
- The introduction of each speaker by the preceding speaker lent to the overall flow of the event and really helped to "build" to the introduction of the Bishop.
- The arrangement of the various events in the program was excellent. The only transition that was a bit awkward was from the puppets to one of the Perkins professors (sorry, but I can't recall her name).

- The mixture of music, with the more contemporary songs in the prelude to the more traditional during the ceremony itself, was wonderful. Jackie and Isaac, were, of course, great. But I loved the choir most of all. It was all so beautiful.

- The puppets were phenomenal! What a light and fun "interlude" during the service. It helped to "break the ice" and let the audience know that it was okay to laugh and enjoy the occasion, as well as learn from it. The best kind of worship, in my opinion! And, since God wants us to worship for ourselves but also for His enjoyment, I have to think that God REALLY enjoyed the worshiping going on Sunday!

- Love, love, love the liturgical dance. Again, the variety encompassed in the program was amazing. There was something for everyone. And for many, there was everything.

- Time structure was respected. I was blown away at how quickly the time went by. At 6pm, when the service ended right on time, I could not believe that I had been there for 3 hours. That is due, in large part, to the excellent organization that went into not only planning the event but in executing it! GREAT JOB!!

Audience Reaction:

- Blown away. Eye opening.
  Humbling. Exhilarating. Challenging. Get-up-off-my-rear-and-do-something excitement! Hopeful.

- Across the board, everyone I spoke with after the event was blown away by the worship experience. It was in a word, amazing. I believe the cornerstones for some bridges were laid on Sunday! Awareness was heightened of not our differences between cultures but our similarities! There are TONS of them. I wish everyone I know could have been there. I wish we could do the same worship at every church in the North Texas area – AME, UMC, Baptist, Church of Christ, Episcopalian, Catholic – doesn't matter. We are all THE CHURCH! Loved that about the diversity emphasis of the whole afternoon. The overriding message of the afternoon, for me at least, was hope. And the feeling that this is really a grassroots endeavor – the bridge building starts with one person reaching out to another person <u>where they are, not where we are</u>. We don't have to wait for "the church" or "the government" or "the schools" or our neighbor. Each of us can do this!!

Responses I Heard:

- Oops. Got a bit ahead of myself. Answered this question in the previous question. To recap, what I heard were comments like:

"That was amazing!"

"I'm just blown away!"

"What an eye-opening experience!"

"How humbling was that?!"

"Going to go bridge building!"

Observations in Response to Bishop's Talk:

Oh my gosh!!!!!!!! I have never heard someone rattle off so much information so quickly, but in such an easy way to follow, grasp and retain. I have so many "catch words" embedded in my brain from her message, and I didn't take one note! Whosoever, howsoever, wheresoever, whensoever. Good news, which I will never think of in the same way again! Powerful, oh so powerful! Her delivery style is so engaging and non-preachy, that I felt she was talking *with* me, rather than *to* me. Although her intellect is obviously off the charts, she has a way of relating to and reaching everyone in the room, regardless of their gender, ethnicity, age. The folks around me were equally fixed on her every word. This was probably due to the passion and sincerity with which she spoke. Texas is blessed beyond measure to have someone like this Bishop standing up and fighting for those who feel they have no voice or no power or no support. If I were going into "the ring," I would definitely want her on my side.

F.   Dear Rev. Ella:

I don't know you very well but have heard great things about you and heard you preach and speak through Emmaus which I've only been connected with since my walk in Sept 2011. However, I was looking forward to attending the service with my friends Kay Carroll and Brenda Davis who are great friends of yours and praise you highly. We arrived about 30 minutes early so the music group was setting up when we arrived and most of the Church greeters had not arrived yet. So, we had an opportunity to hand out programs, offering envelopes and greet people as they arrived. What a blessing.

We intended to leave early, because of Disciple classes at our church (First Frisco) so we sat on the very last back row. I noticed that the audience was mostly divided with our church and mostly their group in front with the others separated and in the back. At the last minute the music group was moved however, all started on time, but the microphones and speakers didn't seem to be working correctly at first.

Then Kay was called forward to the front to take a message to others about the starting of procession. By this time, I was feeling that it was a little disorganized. However, the procession of speakers came in and were seated in a very orderly manner and then the service began.

The very first thing you did during your greeting, that I remember and was really impressed with, was to call us mix and remove the separation and division between our groups. You did it in such a gentle and laughing manner that everyone felt comfortable about moving out of their comfort zone and reaching out to meet new unknown and possibly different people. I moved down towards the front; I loved it and met and sat with some lovely ladies from St. Luke's and saw many others do the same. I felt everyone relax at that point.

The Service was wonderful. The pastors stayed on target, delivering their part of the service in a loving, professional, timely manner. I believe the audience enjoyed each speaker and their personal delivery.

I wasn't sure about what to expect from the Puppet Ministry, but it was delightful and a humorous, joyful break in the service. They performed well, and I thoroughly enjoyed them. The choir and the singers were outstanding, as was to be expected.

I am an older lady with a Southern Baptist background and I am just now becoming accustomed to Spiritual Dancing, so I was amazed at how moved I was by the dancers and music. The youngest dancer especially moved me, with her display of strength with the music. My eyes actually watered with the interpretation of the music by both dancers and those around me seemed to experience the same emotions by wiping away tears and making comments of appreciation during and after the dancing.

Last but certainly not least, the Bishop gave a wonderful sermon. She preached intelligently and with passion. I heard phrases such as "building bridges" coming together. I was really impressed with not only her message, but her delivery and preaching style. I heard others comment on how impressed they were by her message.

Needless to say, we did not leave early but stayed for the entire moving service. Thank you for the wonderful time of sharing God's love and bringing us all closer to Him. I can't remember a service that had so much of an impact on me and I believe others were also truly touched by His Hand through your work.

With God's Blessings
Pam Harvey

Perspective:

From AME Church, Garland
I believe the
sermonic aim was
to never lose focus
of the compassion
and love Jesus
has for people.
His love should
always be the
center of all we
do as
leaders.

Appendix Four – Advisory Team Overview

of Ella McDonald's Preaching

A. <u>Survey of Preaching</u>

I don't remember exactly when I met Reverend Ella McDonald. I know it was in the 1990's, it was at the Lake Sharon Retreat Center in Corinth, Texas, and it was definitely at a Candlelight service for the Walk to Emmaus. She was leading worship and had just delivered the message for the night's worship service. I can't tell you what that message was, but I can say that my husband and I were blown away by the relevance of the message and the passion with which the message was delivered. We both knew that night that this woman was someone special, someone set apart by God to be his servant and messenger in today's world.

My path and Reverend McDonald's continued to cross over those years in the late 1990's and mostly because of our shared passion for service through the Walk to Emmaus. Over the years I had the privilege of serving the community of faith as a member of an Emmaus team where oftentimes Ella served as either the Spiritual Director of the Walk or as an Assistant Spiritual Director. Her talks on those weekends were always filled with stories that brought the message of that talk to life and exuded her love of God and

God's calling on her life. The women on these weekend events (mostly Caucasian) seemed to gravitate towards Ella especially when there were times set apart for spiritual counseling or one-on-one time with a spiritual director. It was not uncommon to see ladies waiting patiently for their turn to talk to Ella. It has always been clear that Ella McDonald's number one priority in her life is her love for and dedication to Jesus Christ, her Lord and Savior; we could all see that.

In 2001, I was elected to the Board of Director for the Dallas Emmaus Community and was thrilled to learn that I would be spending the next three years serving on the board with Reverend Ella McDonald. I came to love those monthly fourth Monday meetings at University Park United Methodist Church where we, as a board, gathered to celebrate Holy Communion before we convened into our regular meeting. As the Community Spiritual Director, Ella would preside over the worship service. I looked forward to her messages on those evenings because I routinely gleaned more from her 10-minute homilies than I did the previous Sunday at my own church. Ella McDonald is so gifted a preacher, her Biblical knowledge so vast and complete, that she is able to provide a theologically sound, meaningful, heart-felt message on the fly, and she is so adept at tailoring that message to her audience. Her prayers, too, are powerful always seeming to touch on something that I needed to ask God for or to thank him for. It was often said that you knew you'd been prayed for when Ella prayed.

As Ella and I got to know each other better, I began to visit her at her church, Agape Temple in southeast Dallas. At the time the members of Ella's church were meeting in a very old church building that was literally falling apart. God placed on Ella's heart that they needed to build a new church. Reverend McDonald saw a need in her community and sought a way to provide a means to an end...that of building a church where the people could gather to praise and worship God. Ella put her faith and trust in the Lord to provide the means to that end, and members from the Emmaus Community, as well as other churches, came together to help provide that community a house of worship. My husband and I joined work teams from our church to help with the construction of the current Agape Temple building. Ella lives her faith everyday...she is definitely one who not only "talks the talk but walks the walk."

I have spent many Sundays sitting in the pews at Reverend McDonald's church (whether at her current church – the AME where she has served as senior pastor since 2011, or former church – Agape Temple AME where she served as pastor from 1991 until 2011) worshipping with her congregation. And I have sat in my own church when she preached there. Every time I hear Ella preach, the message is tailor-made for her audience. In my mostly Caucasian, United Methodist church her messages have always been based strictly on scripture with a lesson and a story to illustrate the point – more intellectually based. My experience in her AME church has been that the message, while based on scripture with stories from real life to illustrate the point, is geared towards reaching the heart of those listening and thus elicits an emotional response to the Word. "Hallelujahs" and "Amens" resound throughout the hall in her AME church. It is so obvious that Ella's congregation loves her and that she loves them as well. Reverend McDonald is a blessing to all who have the privilege of knowing her and are able to hear her preach God's word and His will for our lives.

Susan Crowell

B. Survey of Preaching

Hello, my name is LaNita Rainwater and I am a former member and ordained deacon of Agape Temple AME Church. Where Rev. Ella M. McDonald was my pastor and mentor for 10 years.

I have had the awesome duty and privilege over the years to serve and observe Pastor McDonald as she ministered to countless number of people, of various churches of, ethnic, social and economic backgrounds as well as in Prisons and on Retreats throughout the state of Texas.

She is no respecter or persons when it comes to preaching and teaching the gospel of Jesus Christ.

Though she is often thought of as a simple, meek and mild-mannered person to the natural eye this couldn't be more further from the truth when she stands to deliver the word of God. She not only commands her audience attention with her creative expressions that bring the word to life and her powerful biblical insight, the anointing of God upon her gives life to lost souls, offers hope to the weary and mends the brokenhearted, all while leading them to the throne of God!

I have seen the repentant who have struggled in drugs and alcohol shake and tremble as they fall in her arms weeping, asking what must I do to be saved?

I have witnessed her stop teaching bible study and minister to an abused two-year-old who walked right up to her and would only be held by Pastor McDonald. As she suffered not the little children to come unto to her for such is the kingdom of God.

I have witnessed both men and women answer the clarion call to ministry after she has preached on servant hood.

I have observed the masses stand to thunderous applauses with Halleluiahs and Amens while others simply looked on with jaw dropping amazement at her sound Christian theology and revelations!

In conclusion, some may only see her as a black woman who preaches the gospel. Some as a Pastor of congregations and other's as a great orator of her time…But I see Jesus.

C. My Impressions of Rev. Ella McDonald's Ministry

I met Rev. Ella McDonald about 10 years ago at my church's women's retreat. I had heard many great things about her prior to our finally meeting. However, nothing could prepare me for the impact Rev. Ella would have on my spiritual life, on the women who attended that retreat and future retreats, and countless others in the Emmaus, Kairos, and Epiphany Communities.

Following that first retreat, my primarily Caucasian church invited, or more accurately insisted, that Rev. Ella speak at each of its yearly women's retreats since. Our church began inviting women from all area churches to attend its annual women's retreats. Soon thereafter other churches began asking Rev. Ella to lead their women's retreats. In addition, our church asked her to preach its revival several years ago, and we received very favorable feedback from those attending.

I have also had the privilege of serving on numerous Walk to Emmaus weekends with Rev. Ella. I would venture that her devotion to this and other similar three-day ecumenical Christian movements (such as Kairos, Kairos Outside, and Epiphany) is unparalleled among her peers. Plus, I have visited Rev. Ella's churches and heard her preach in her "home" environment.

In each and every one of those situations, Rev. Ella's passion for sharing the message God placed on her heart was evident to all and enthusiastically received. Her knowledge of the Word is exceptional, and her theologically sound messages are tremendously well received. However, her ability to draw on real-life stories and examples to bring the scriptures vividly to life in the minds and understanding of her audiences makes her truly special. I once heard her use something as simple as popcorn to brilliantly make a point when sharing a message prior to administering Holy Communion.

Moreover, celebrating The Lord's Supper with Rev. Ella forever changed my appreciation of sharing such a glorious meal. Rev. Ella invokes such gratitude for what Our Savior did for all on the cross that I now approach Holy Communion with a completely different heart.

In each setting, regardless of the demographics (age, ethnicity, gender, etc.) of the audience, the setting of the event, or the topic of her message, Rev. Ella has the ability to bridge the gaps between God in the pages of the Bible and God in each attendee's life, between the historical events of the scripture and the real-life events in their lives, and most amazingly between the attendees themselves. Whenever and wherever Rev. Ella speaks with the authority of the Holy Spirit, He infuses her with His power, insight and love. When that happens, race, color, age and gender are, Praise the Lord! completely irrelevant.

Respectfully submitted by,
Nancy Summers
First United Methodist Church, Royse City

D. My Impressions of the Ministry of Rev. Ella McDonald

My name is Cathy Partridge, and I am a Local Pastor in the North Texas Conference of the United Methodist Church and currently serve under appointment at First United Methodist Church of Frisco, but that has not always been the case. My first memory of encountering Pastor Ella was around the end of 1998 when she came to be a guest preacher at a large, almost exclusively Caucasian United Methodist Church in the Dallas/Fort Worth metroplex. The presiding pastor was out on a retreat and had asked Pastor Ella to take his pulpit for the morning. I still remember her saying that she was used to preaching for three hours on a given Sunday morning, but not three one-hour worship services. Ella talked that Sunday about her call to ministry, the personal sacrifice and lasting impact of leaving her position as a math teacher to follow God's will for her life. I specifically recall her speaking about how, when she was a teacher, she had a closet full of shoes and now she had one pair of shoes, but that she wouldn't have it any other way. Almost 15 years later I can still remember her message, and I have returned to that witness of self-sacrifice more often than I can count over the years, and especially after I began exploring my call to ministry.

Since 1998 I cannot even recall how many times I have heard Pastor Ella preach and speak, and the majority of those times have been in a predominately Caucasian, United Methodist setting. I personally have invited Ella to lead at least ten women's retreats where she would preach and teach three or four sessions over a weekend. There is one women's group that has invited her back year after year for over ten years which illustrates to me how relevant and timely her messages are and how engaging and contagious her preaching style is to people of all ages.

Ella also led a three-day church revival several years ago at a time in which that particular congregation needed a biblically solid and passionate message of hope and healing. I don't know of another person, male or female, black or white, who could have done a more spectacular and effective job. Through Pastor Ella, the Holy Spirit showed up and revived and empowered. Again, this congregation was almost exclusively Caucasian, and the context is a small town, primarily farming and bedroom community; and still her messages were not only well received, but life changing.

Throughout the years I have also served on a great number of Walk to Emmaus weekends with Ella. The Walk to Emmaus is an ecumenical retreat movement that reaches people of all ages, faith experiences and personal backgrounds. I served with Ella from the lay side, before I went into ministry, and then again for several years as a fellow clergy person. I would venture to say that Ella is the most highly respected and requested clergy in the Dallas Emmaus community. Like E.F. Hutton, if Pastor Ella is speaking, everyone wants to listen!

As a friend, I know how much time and effort Ella puts into every talk, message, sermon and presentation she makes. I have seen Ella work for hours on a talk she has given twenty times before. Each time she speaks, it is based on sound theological doctrine and her gifted insight into the scriptures. Her passion and love for Christ not only comes through but is contagious. I can confidently say that I have seen Ella in enough settings and enough individual times that her preaching style is not only universally accepted, but desired and sought after. I have told her often, when I grow up, I want to be Pastor Ella – but alas, I know that will never happen.

E. Evaluation of Ministry of Pastor Ella M. McDonald, February 27, 2014

I have been a member of two churches Pastored by Rev. Ella McDonald, and offer the following evaluation of her ministry:

• The ministry of Pastor McDonald would be described by me as a very solid ministry. Pastor McDonald's ministry is consistent, preached and taught with authority and assurance that she knows what she is preaching and/or teaching about. A ministry that brings people in, desiring to understand God's Word and desiring to be a part of the ministry. Pastor McDonald's ministry is a ministry often filled with hope, life experiences, world events, personal journeys she has experienced, love, realness and certainly of biblical context.

- As a former member of Agape Temple African Methodist Episcopal Church, I was under the leadership of Pastor McDonald for 10 years and have heard her preach, speak, and teach on several occasions. Over these 10 years, I heard her preach at least 3-4 Sunday's per month, and would say the same with our weekly teaching sessions. She taught weekly bible study sessions at least 3 – 4 times per month every year. Her Sunday Morning sermons are always very well prepared, always seem to relate to current situations and/or life experiences and are preached in such a manner that the text given often before she preaches is explained in a way that leads to a better understanding of the preached word she gives. In other words, because Pastor McDonald quiet often exegesis the text she is preaching from, or gives an illustration of the text, before going into the actual sermon, I find that it allows clarity of the scripture that is being taught and discussed. My analysis of this process that I have become used to receiving over these 12 plus years, is that by explaining the text and teaching the text it helps fully understand the lessons being taught. This is a very effective process as it helps the listeners understand and relate to ministry and God's word.

- In addition to being under her leadership as my Pastor and hearing her preach and teach as members of the church, I was given the opportunity to be a part of an Emmaus Walk for women. This Emmaus Walk was attended by several women, and I was the only one from my church attending at this time. Pastor McDonald served as the Spiritual Director during this retreat. In evaluating Pastor McDonald's style of teaching I would use descriptive adjectives such as: prepared, knowledgeable, concise, purposeful, and structured.

Pastor McDonald knows what she teaches!! Her study of the Word shows whenever she preaches or teaches! Again, not only does she teach from what the scripture reads, but she breaks it down so that it is taught with much clarity.

- As a longtime member of two churches under Pastor McDonald's pastoral leadership, I have attended at least 4 retreats over the years where I have witnessed Pastors McDonald speak at these retreats. She speaks with holy boldness and assurance! In reiteration, her delivery of speeches, sermons, and teachings are always given with clarity to God's word, and as she would call them, often delivered with "sidebars" – which are almost always rhetorical and humorous. The aim is for the audience to reach an act of faith based on God's word.

- Although our church is predominantly African American, we have several Hispanic/Caucasian families who are faithful and dedicated members. They ministry style that Pastor McDonald administers is a ministry not geared toward racial ethnicity, it is a ministry that reaches the people.

- I have attended at least 10 or more worship services with Caucasian churches over the years where Pastor McDonald preached. My witness to this is that racial ethnicity does not bear much on her ministry; it does not determine 'how she preaches', but it is taken into consideration with her preparation to preach to diverse congregation. The structure of her delivering a theological, sound, logical, and precise Word is always given – regardless of the ethnicity of the congregation. The African American, Hispanic, Caucasian congregations that I have witnessed her preach before all receive, regardless of ethnicity, sound doctrine – as described in Titus 2:1 and paraphrased as "teach to be worthy of respect, self-controlled, and sound in faith, in love and in endurance." Pastor McDonald's theological preaching, speaking, and teaching exemplifies Paul's conversation about delivering sound doctrine inclusive of "self-control, love, patience, and full of faith".

- Pastor McDonald's passion for preaching is evident in her daily journey. She carries God's Word with her and will share it with whether in church, or outside of church. I served as one of her officers for several years, and the Steward Board which I served on was charged with being aware of the Pastor's well-being in both personal life and ministry. Because of her passion to minister, she would go tirelessly without taking a vacation. On a few occasions, the board members would have to encourage her to take time for herself and take a vacation. Her passion for ensuring members were feed God's Word continually would sometimes cause her to preach/teach for weeks without taking a break for herself. She realizes the importance of taking care of herself, but because she is so passionate about the calling that God has given her, she puts ministry first. Dedicated to ministry would be a good way to speak about her.

- I would say if you asked anyone, members or non-members how they felt about Pastor's biblical knowledge, their response, and mine, would be that biblical knowledge is what she knows; biblical knowledge is what she preaches; biblical knowledge is what she teaches. In Bible Study or Sunday School teachings, we have opportunities to discuss the lesson and give input, and opportunities to ask questions. Pastor's exegetical biblical text is phenomenon! She is very knowledgeable of biblical text and because of this, it strengthens her ability to preach, speak, teach the Word.

- In the many settings I have had the honored opportunity to see and hear Pastor McDonald preach, speak, and/or teach, I observed the audience be captivated by the message she delivers; I have observed the audience understanding what they are accepting when they come forth to become Christians; I have observed relationships, friendships, marriages, hurtfulness, and sorrows being comforted and healed; I have observed forgiveness among the people; I have observed young and old committing their lives to Christ.

- In closing, my observation and evaluation of context and beyond of the Pastor McDonald's ministry is that it is a ministry consistently filled with the Word of God, delivered by a servant who it truly Called by God.

Thanking you for taking the time to receive my observation and evaluation feedback.

Dianna Thompson

E. Reverend Ella Mae McDonald

Respectfully Submitted By: Cynthia Wilson

As I consider all the things I can say about Rev. Ella McDonald, I would first have to say, it is a privilege to have an opportunity to speak on her behalf, and one I do not take lightly nor without a great deal of thought. Because, I have such a high regard for this woman of God, I found myself taking a deep breath and then praying for the exact words. A woman who is no nonsense when it comes to serving God and being obedient to His word. A woman who is extremely passionate about her calling. A woman who is serious about Gods vision for her ministry. A woman who is steadfast and unmovable in her love for God and her faith. Her compassion for God's people and leading them into a right relationship with Him is unwavering.

My very first time hearing this pastor preach was in 1993, at an Annual Conference in the African Methodist Episcopal Church. I've heard numerous sermons preached by numerous pastors, but when I heard Rev. McDonald preach, it truly left a lasting effect on me spiritually. I had never seen or heard a preacher, let alone a female preacher, preach like this woman! She had everyone, from the choir stand to the backdoors standing to their feet. She was on fire and so were the people! I could not believe, that through the Holy Spirit, this short woman of statue was able to captivate her listeners, in that she was able to fine-tune her sermon in such a way that it was relatable to every age group in that sanctuary. It was a memorable experience for me, and one that would change my life forever.

Although, I was not a member of Rev. McDonald's church at the time, I often thought about her through the years. As fate would have it, in 2003, I made the tough decision to leave the church I had called home for many years and one I loved dearly. I transferred my membership to sit under her leadership and teaching. This is how much she touched my life, and after hearing her preach only once! The enthusiasm she displays when preaching and teaching the word of God is so profound! In our church, she continues to inspire, lead, challenge and motivate us. A prime example is how she balances her rigorous schedule; her obligations to the church, her members, the AMEC, district and conference wide, the countless retreats and her sometimes challenging classes. She demonstrates that all things are obtainable through Christ!

Having sat under this pastor's leadership for more than ten years, I have witnessed the many hats she so graciously wears. She's not only a devoted pastor and leader in the African Methodist Episcopal Church (AMEC), but she is also well known, loved and respected in the United Methodist Church (UMC). This group of people, mainly Caucasian, is very much a part of her personal life and ministry. Before she even stands to open her mouth, you can see the enthusiasm and reverence they have for this lady.

They are overjoyed when opportunity permits them to see her, to hear her preach, speak, sing, teach, etc.! Rev. McDonald, along with our church has been invited to attend and participate in countless events in the UMC, where she is most often the guest preacher. To say our Caucasian brothers and sisters have a warm spot in their hearts for this woman of God is stating it mildly. Their admiration for this lady goes beyond words and belief.

For instance: In their normal setting, where they are usually less vocal and more reserved, it is just the opposite when she is preaching in their venue or even that of another location where they are present. Watching them transform right before my eyes is almost like seeing their alter ego's come out. I have seen their faces flushed and I have seen them "High Five" the person(s) sitting next to them. I've watched them through the years become more involved, more expressive and more interactive when it comes to Rev. McDonald. Because of their love and commitment to God and the esteem they have for this pastor, our Caucasian brothers and sisters continues to show their love and support towards this woman of God personally and in her ministry.

A huge part of Rev. McDonald's life is the spiritual retreats she's involved in. They are important to her, as she participates in an unlimited number throughout the year. Anyone who knows her understands how significant they are to her. I have not participated in many spiritual retreats; however, the ones I have been blessed to be part of, were moments I will not soon forget! During and after her preaching or teaching segments, I have seen women who were hurting for whatever reason, find healing and release. Women, who were unsure of their life's path, are given hope and a sense of direction. Women who have low self-esteem seems to gain a self-respect or self-awareness that they never knew existed.

It goes without saying that I could go on talking about the countless ways this woman of God has touched so many lives. These retreats are both powerful and much needed. She does an excellent job at nourishing souls that are in desperate need. Rev. McDonald makes you feel as though you are the only one in the room, the only one that matters. She just has a way of making you believe you can do anything, which stands to reason why the retreats are so successful and such a big deal. One of her strong suits is that she is never judgmental. Somehow, she makes you feel like she has walked in your shoes even though she has not.

As I reflect over my time spent listening and watching Pastor McDonald and her unique style, it is no wonder so many Christians and Non-Christians are drawn to her. This woman's level of integrity goes beyond what most can even appreciate! Her singing and the use of her famous *"Sidebar"* humor captures the audience attention. Rev. McDonald's priority is to please God, which is obvious in the way she carries herself and, in the way, she leads her congregation and others. When preaching, it is always evident that she has put in the work, an adequate amount of time in preparing her sermons.

I appreciate the fact that she does not rush when preaching the word, but literally takes her time. She gives thought provoking sermon topics, which are in sync with her Scripture text and Key Points. It is not hard to follow her messages because she will not leave one point without explaining it in detail. Speaking for myself and those I have sat in worship with, I can truly say we are usually in awe at this lady. At times, when her messages become so deep, I literally must sit back and watch her do her thing. The level of energy this woman has is absolutely amazing. Although, there is an audience to preach to, sometimes she even preaches her own self happy!

Rev. McDonald can lay out a Scripture like no one I've ever heard. The exhilaration and wisdom she brings to the platform is profound! She is truly set apart. Whereas, it may take another pastor ten or twenty minutes to warm-up to a congregation or get into "worship mode", it is completely opposite for her, and it doesn't matter the scenario, {preaching, reviewing a Sunday School lesson or simply giving an example of a discussion at the time}.

In my opinion, Rev. McDonald exemplifies the Scripture *"study to show yourself approved unto God"*, as she has and continues to give God's people her best! She is very strategic in her presentations, in that she never begins a sermon without prayer, without asking God to remove "Ella", or decrease "Ella" and increase God, so the people may see Him rather than her. Even after years of preaching, I think she still gets nervous and anxious, which in my opinion is a good thing. Being anxious when delivering any form of God's word, is one of her strongest attributes. By that I mean, she recognizes that without God she can do nothing; thus, she is able to remain humble.

I also believe because she does have a humble spirit, she has favor with God beyond what she can even comprehend; therefore, she is able to deliver messages of hope, messages of deliverance and messages of healing. By having this strength, it enables her to go forth with what God has given her to give to us. When she stands to deliver God's message, she is prayed up and ready! Her knowledge of the Scriptures continues to astonish me. For example: If you're having a conversation with her or needs prayer, you better be ready because she's going to either throw in a Scripture or follow up with one. Her love and obedience to God is unyielding, and it goes beyond the pulpit! It goes beyond the walls of the church!

Rev. McDonald is determined to give the people what they need rather than what they desire. She preaches sermons that provide sustenance and a lasting effect. Sermons that help build our faith level. Sermons that carry us from one crisis to the next. Sermons that teach us to focus on God rather than the crisis itself. Sermons that help build our character. Sermons that cause us to dig deeper for God's purpose in our lives. So, it is no surprise that while preaching, if she feels we have missed an important fact, she will gladly transition into her famous *"Sidebar"* tactics. She basically does whatever it takes to gain our attention, in order that we may gain the full understanding.

She often makes this statement to the congregation: "I love you too much to send you to hell", which is why she does not pamper us, but presents us with sermons that often are not too popular with most. While this challenge hasn't always been easy for her, because she does have such a caring heart where her members are concerned; nevertheless, she has made the shift rather well.

This deep woman of God is intense! She knows the word of God and discerns how to dissect it to the point that no one should leave her congregation or gathering misunderstood. A notable strength of Rev. McDonald is that of consistency, and I believe it's because she understands the enormous impact she has on the people she shepherds and beyond. Another strength is that she can distinguish what the people's needs are; hence, she is able to draw them in, hold their attention and feed them accordingly. I think for this reason, she does study the word of God diligently and extensively, to not short change her listeners.

The people are fascinated by her tone, her gestures, her attentiveness, her knowledge of the Word, her delivery of the Word, her holy boldness, her compassion and her honesty! The look on some people's face as Rev. McDonald moves further into her message is one of amazement. You can see the tears of joy, tears of relief, the laughter, and even a look by many that say "okay, now I can go a little further on this journey" or "wow, I get it". It is truly something to see and appreciate.

When members of the congregation come together, and they seemingly get the point or points she is trying to relay, she gets totally involved, almost as if she is having an out of body experience! If the Spirit is moving uncontrollably, she may break out in song, dance or a shout. It is awesome to watch! Essentially, what it comes down to is, when there is positive feedback from the congregation, and they grasp how excited and involved the pastor is, I believe it echoes to them that although she is our Shepard, she is still a vessel of God; hence, she still has feelings and emotions just like the rest of us, and yes, she knows how to praise and worship God in the Spirit and in the Truth.

It is evident that when the congregation is totally participating in the worship experience, they can see and perhaps almost feel Rev. McDonald's dedication, authenticity, hunger and adoration. People, as well as myself are absolutely blown away by this woman of God!

And, it's not that we don't see God in her, it's because we do see Him all over and around her! God's power and presence flows through her, which becomes a chain reaction or as she has put it in a past sermon, we hopefully are becoming *"Change Agents"*. Wow!!

Grant you, most people would probably ask how is it possible for a person to have so many positive qualities, yet no flaws? Well, I must admit Rev. McDonald does have some imperfections; although they would be considered minor to some. If I had to list her weaknesses, I would have to say it is her compassion, commitment level and her love for God's people. Where, I don't feel there is anything wrong with having compassion because I too suffer with this quality; however, Rev. McDonald will literally give anyone the shirt off her back. She will give her last dime to anyone in need, and if God has spoken in her Spirit to give some random person money, etc., she does it and without hesitation. I understand it is better to give than to receive; but, I don't know if there is a limit to how far she will go.

Likewise, her commitment level is absolutely amazing. She goes and goes and goes! Commitment is great, as I believe everyone should pride them self on following through with commitments. Nonetheless, Rev. McDonald goes a step further with this as well. If her calendar is full to capacity and someone ask her to preach for an annual day, a spiritual retreat, etc., she will find a way to add it to the calendar. The simple fact is, she does not like to say no to anyone! Her heart cannot take it!! It does not matter if she is sick either; because once the seed has been planted in her mind, she will usually find a way to work things out. For so long she has put others first and herself last.

My prayer is that God will continue to show her how to balance her schedule, personal and otherwise, as to not neglect Rev. McDonald, the person. Lastly, but certainly not least; the love Rev. McDonald has for God's people is almost unbelievable. Like I stated earlier, she has a way of making you feel as though she has walked in your shoes, and maybe because there is no judgment on her part, merely pure love. She sees the positive in everything and the good in everyone. When folks are misleading or spitefully try to hurt her or others, it's almost hard for her to fathom, because she does want to see the good in everyone. My prayer is always for God to guard her mind and especially her heart. So, you see, this woman of God has many wonderful and amazing qualities, and yes, there are a few imperfections as well; although, are they really considered "imperfections"?

In closing, it has been my extreme honor to follow this amazing, hard-working, devoted, compassionate, loving woman of God. To sit under her leadership and learn more than I could have ever imagined, about Christ and myself. To watch her overcome various obstacles, only to see her achieve countless victories. To see her reach her God-given potentials, both personally and spiritually. Rev. McDonald continues to motivate and challenge me, both as a Christian and as a woman. She has shown me and others that you are never too old to pursue a higher education and it is never too late for God's purpose to be revealed or fulfilled. Through her perseverance, faith and obedience, I truly understand for this woman of God the meaning of Jeremiah 29:11: *"For I know the plans I have for you; declares the Lord, plans to prosper you and not to harm you, plans to give you hope and a future."*

Reverend Ella Mae McDonald is a woman after God's own heart, and one who has impacted my life immensely, as well as countless others. I cannot wait to see all the ways God will continue using this called and anointed woman!

Appendix Five

These are the five Churches in which I, Rev. McDonald preached:

An AME Church in Garland, Texas
Sunday July 21, 2013

A UMC in Mabank, Texas
Sunday, July 28, 2013

A UMC in Mesquite, Texas
September 29, 2013

A Local Fellowship Church in Dallas, Texas
October 6, 2013

A Hispanic Church in Dallas, Texas
November 10, 2013

Although the Bulletins are not displayed here in the Book; each Sunday I, Rev. Dr. Ella M. McDonald preached a powerful spirit filled message, and after the Benedictions had gone Forth it was evident the people in the Congregations were blessed, delivered and felt the power of the Holy Spirit radiating in the church.

Question Number Seven - What did you find especially helpful about this sermon?

From UMC Mabank –

Personal illustrations shared about times when you struggled to meet the mortgage, or didn't have a car, etc. Showed a "realness" about Ella, that she KNOWS what it's like to be without and that she can relate to others. Taking the time to stop and sing "He Touched Me." Besides it is fitting right in with the text, it was very moving. I will never again hear that song without it meaning more to me. I can picture Jesus touching me and healing me. The promise that God will heal me and get me to where I'm going is powerful and this song helped with the concept. It gave a moment of reprieve to digest what all had been said and to ponder the words of a very familiar song.

Bibliographies:

This is My Story: Testimonies and Sermons of Black Women in Ministry, edited by La Rue, Cleophus J. Louisville: Westminster John Knox Press, 2005.

Purposes of Preaching, edited by Jana Childers. Atlanta: Chalice Press, 2004.

—— *Relating to People of Other Faiths: Insights from the Bible.* Tiruvalla, India: Christian Sahitya Samithy, 2004.

Alexander, Eric, Beeke, Joel, Boice, James M, Ferguson, Sinclair, Kistler, Don, MacArthur, John, Mohler Albert, Piper, John, Sproul, Jr. R.C., and Thomas, Derek. *Feed My Sheep: A Passionate Plea for Preaching* (Soli Deo Gloria Publishers, Florida 2002)

Allen, Ronald J. *Preaching: An Essential Guide.* Nashville: Abingdon Press 2002.

Bauckham, Richard. *Gospel Women: Studies of the Named Women in the Gospels.* Michigan: William B. Eerdmans Publishing Company, 2002.

Bond, L. Susan. *Contemporary African American Preaching: Diversity in Theory and Style.* Saint Louis: Christian Board of Publication, 2003.

Bristow, John T. *What Paul Really Said About Women*: An Apostle's Liberating Views on Equality in Marriage, Leadership, and Love. Harper, San Francisco 1988.

Brenner, Athalya. *I am: Biblical Women Tell Their Own Stories.* Canada: Augsburg Fortress Press, 2005.

Brosend, William. *The Preaching of Jesus: Gospel Proclamation, Then and Now*. Westminster John Knox Press; 1 edition February 2010.

Carl, William J. III. *Preaching Christian Doctrine*. Philadelphia: Fortress Press, 1984.

Chapell, Bryan. *Christ-Centered Preaching: Redeeming the Expository Sermon*. Baker Press, Grand Rapids, 2005.

Costen, Melva Wilson. *African-American Christian Worship*. Abingdon Press, Nashville 1st edition 1993.

Kim, Eunjoo Mary. *Women Preaching*. Cleveland: Pilgrim Press 2004.

Fabarez, Michael. *Preaching that Changes Lives*. Eugene, OR: Wipf and Stock Publishers, 2002.

Feehan, Fr. James. *Preaching Christ Crucified: Our Guilty Silence*. The Mercier Press, Dublin Irland, 1991.

Florence, Anna Carter. *Preaching as Testimony*. Louisville: Westminster John Knox Press, 2007.

George, Timothy, Massey James Earl and Robert Smith, Jr. *Our Sufficiency Is Of God*. Macon, Georgia.: Mercer University Press, 2010.

Griffin, David R. *Varieties in Postmodern Theology*. New York: U. of N.Y. Press, 1989.

Hall, Edward T. *Beyond Culture*. Doubleday Anchor Books, New York 1977.

Hatch, G. L. "*Logic in the Black Folk Sermon: The Sermons of Rev. C. L. Franklin,*" Journal of Black Studies 26 (1996): Nashville: Abingdon Press, 1989.

House, Wayne H. *The Role of Women in Ministry Today*. Nashville, Tennessee: Thomas Nelson Publishers, 1990.

Jewett, Paul K. *Man as Male and Female.* Grand   Rapids, Eerdmans,

1975.

Kalas, J. Ellsworth. *Strong Was Her Faith: Women of the New Testament.* Nashville, Abingdon Press, 2007.

Keener, Craig S. *Paul, Women, & Wives: Marriage and Women's Ministry in the Letters of Paul. Peabody, MA: Henderson, 1992.*

Kalas, J. Ellsworth. *Preaching From The Soul:* Nashville, Abingdon Press, 2003.

Kung, Hans. *Theology for the Third Millennium.* New York: Anchor Books, 1988.

Lancaster, Sara Heaner. *Women and the Authority of Scripture.* New York: T&T Clark, 2001.

Lapsley, Jacqueline. *Whispering the Word: Hearing Women's Stories in the Old Testament.* Nashville: Westminster john Knox Press: 2005.

La Rue, Cleophus J. *I Believe I'll Testify: The Art of African American Preaching.* Louisville: Westminster John Knox Press, 2011.

Letham, Robert. *The Holy Trinity in Scripture, History, Theology, and Worship.* Phillipsburg, NJ: P&R, 2004.

Lincoln, C. Eric and Lawrence H. Mamiya. *The Black Church in the African American Experience.*   North Carolina: Duke University Press, 1990.

Lingenfelter, Judith and Sherwood. *Teaching Cross Culturally.* Grand Rapids MI: Baker Academic Publisher, 2003.

Long, Thomas G. *The Witness of Preaching.* Louisville: Westminster John Knox Press, 1989.

Madhu, Dubey. *Black Women Novelists and the Nationalist Aesthetic*. Bloomington: Indiana University Press, 1994.

Madhu, Dubey. *Signs and Cities: Black Literary Postmodernism*. Chicago and London: University of Chicago Press, 2003.

Malphurs, Aubrey. *Planting Growing Churches for the 21st Century*. Baker Books, MI, 1998.

Massey, J. E. *Designing the Sermon: Order and Movement in Preaching*. Nashville: Abingdon, 1980.

McGee, Lee. *Wrestling with the Patriarchs: Retrieving Women's Voices in Preaching*. Nashville: Abingdon Press 1996.

McKenzie, Alyce M. *Preaching Proverbs: Wisdom for the Pulpit*. Louisville, KY: Westminster John Knox Press, 1996.

McKenzie, Alyce M. *Preaching Biblical Wisdom in a Self-Help Society*. Nashville: Abingdon, 2002.

McKenzie, Alyce M. *Hear and Be Wise: Becoming a Teacher and Preacher of Wisdom*. Louisville, KY: Westminster John Knox Press, 2007.

McKenzie, Vashti M. *Not without Strength: Leadership Developments for African American Women in Ministry*. Cleveland, OH: United Church Press, 1996.

McKenzie, Vashti M. *Strength in the Struggle*. Cleveland, OH: The Pilgrim Press, 2001.

McKenzie, Vashti M. *Journey to the Well*. New York: Penguin Group USA Inc. 2002.

McKenzie, Vashti Murphy. *Those Sisters Can Preach: 22 Pearls of Wisdom, Virtue and Hope*. The Pilgrim Press, Cleveland, Ohio 2013.

McKnight, Edgar V. *Postmodern Uses of the Bible*. Nashville: Abingdon Press, 1988.

Mohler, R. Albert Jr. *A Theology of Preaching, Handbook of Contemporary Preaching*. Michael Duduitt, ed., Nashville: Broadman Press, 1992.

Moyd, Olin P. *The Sacred Art: Preaching & Theology in the African American Tradition* (Judson Press, 1995).

Neuhaus, John. *Freedom of Ministry*. Grand Rapids, MI: Eerdmans, 1979.

Newbigin, Lesslie. *Foolishness to the Greeks*. Grand Rapids: Eerdmans Publ. Co., 1986. NIV Study Bible. Grand Rapids: Zondervan, 1985.

Nieman, James and Rogers, Thomas. *Preaching to Every Pew, Cross Cultural Strategies for Preaching*. Philadelphia: Fortress Press, 2001.

Reeves, Michael. *Delighting in the Trinity: An Introduction to the Christian Faith*, Downers Grove, IL, InterVarsity Press, 2012.

Reinhold, Ponder and Michele Tuck- Ponder. *The Wisdom Of The Word Love: Great African-American Sermons*. New York, New York.: Crown Publishers, Inc., 1997.

Soards, Marion L. *The Speeches in Acts: Their Content, Context and Concern*. Louisville, Westminster John Knox, 1994.

Sookhdeo, Patrick ed. *Jesus Christ the Only Way: Christian Responsibility in a Multicultural Society*. Exeter, UK: The Paternoster Press. 1978.

Steffen, Thomas A. and Hasslegrave, David J. *Reconnecting God's Story to ministry: Cross Cultural storytelling at Home and Abroad*, La Habra: Center for Organization and Ministry, 1997; quoted in Stetzer, *Planting Missional Churches*, (Broadman and Holman Publishing, Nashville, TN. 2006.

Stewart, C. F. *Soul Survivors: An African American Spirituality.* Louisville, KY: Westminster John Knox Press, 1997.

Taylor, Gardner C. *Chariots of Fire.* Nashville, Tennessee: Broadman Press, 1988.

Taylor, Gardner C. *Faith In The Fire: Wisdom For Life.* Taylor, Edward T. ed. New York, New York: Smiley Books Publisher, 2011.

Taylor Richard, L. *The Words Of Gardner Taylor*: Volume 1. Valley Forge, Pennsylvania: Judson Press, 1999.

Thiselton, Anthony C. *The Two Horizons.* Grand Rapids: Eerdmans, 1980.

Thomas, Frank A. *They Like to Never Quit Praisin' God.* Cleveland; The Pilgrim Press, 1997.

Thomas, Gerald Lamont. *African American Preaching: The Contribution of Dr. Gardner C. Taylor.* New York, New York.: Peter Lang Publishing, Inc., 2004.

Thomas, Robert L. *Introduction to Exegesis.* Sun Valley: author, 1987.

Tisdale, Nora Tubbs. *Prophetic Preaching: A Pastoral Approach.* Louisville, KY: Westminster John Knox Press, 2010.

Turner, Mary Donovan and Hudson, Mary. Lin. *Saved from Silence: Finding Women's Voices in Preaching.* Atlanta: Chalice Press, 1999.

Vanhoozer, Kevin J., Anderson, Charles A., Sleasman, Michael J. *Everyday Theology: How to Read Cultural Texts and*

Interpret Trends. Baker Academic, a division of Baker Publishing Group 2007.

Verdesi, Elizabeth. *In but Still Out.* Pennsylvania: Westminster Press, 1976.

Weems, Renita J. *Reading Her Way through the Struggle: African American Women and the Bible.* In *Stony the Road We Trod,* edited by Cain Hope Felder. Maryknoll, New York: Orbis Books, 1991.

West, Cornel. *Prophetic Fragments.* Grand Rapids, Michigan: Eerdmans, 1988.

Wilmore, Gayraud and Cone, James H. *Black Theology: A Documentary History, 1966-1979.* Maryknoll, New York: Orbis Books, 1979.

Vita

Rev. Ella Mae McDonald received a Bachelor of Science Degree from North Texas State University in 1978, and a Master of Divinity Degree from Southern Methodist University - Perkins School of Theology in 2008. She was licensed to preach in 1980, at St. James African Methodist Episcopal Church (A.M.E) in Denton, Texas. She was ordained an Itinerant Deacon in the African Methodist Episcopal Church October 1982 and was ordained an Itinerant Elder in 1984. Rev. McDonald served as the Pastor of Bethel A.M.E Church in Gainesville, Texas from October 1984 to October 1988. She served as the pastor of Agape Temple AME Church 1988 to November 2010. Presently, she serves as the Pastor of St. Luke AME Church in Garland, Texas.

In order to

gain a hearing

and to overcome the resistances

one faces in gaining

that hearing,

the preacher must remain

faithful to the calling

of revealing what

God has spoken in the Holy Bible.

This is what we have

been called to do,

to express God's glory

in and beyond our

cultural context.